# *The Promise*
# *of*
# *Bultmann*

## *by*
## *NORMAN PERRIN*

FORTRESS PRESS    PHILADELPHIA

COPYRIGHT © 1969 BY NORMAN PERRIN

*First Fortress Press edition 1979*

---

**Library of Congress Cataloging in Publication Data**

Perrin, Norman.
 The promise of Bultmann.

 Reprint of the ed. published by Lippincott,
Philadelphia, in series: The Promise of theology.
 Bibliography: p.
 1. Bultmann, Rudolf Karl, 1884-1976. I. Title.
[BX4827.B78P4 1979]     230′.092′4     78-19639
ISBN 0-8006-1357-0

---

7404I78    Printed in the United States of America    1-1357

# *Contents*

# Foreword

I am very pleased and appreciative that this introduction to Bultmann's accomplishment and intention, written over a six-week period in the summer of 1968 to fulfill an obligation to colleague Martin E. Marty and long out of print, has been given new life.

As a scholar, trained historically in the life and teaching of Jesus, Norman Perrin was very much involved in the debate and dispute about Rudolf Bultmann and the meaning of his teaching. Because he talked about the things he cared about, I feel I can say that in his own personal understanding of the relationship between God and man and the possibilities for human existence in the world, Norman Perrin was most responsive to Bultmann's theology. He considered Bultmann to be the greatest New Testament scholar of the twentieth century, and perhaps the greatest of any century.

NANCY PERRIN

Chicago, Illinois
September 20, 1978

# *Foreword to First Edition*

Rudolf Bultmann has been the greatest New Testament scholar of the twentieth century. So say many of his colleagues and rivals. No, Bultmann has muddied theological waters by tying himself to the tortured philosophy of his fellow Marburger, Martin Heidegger. So say most anti-Heideggerians, and their number is legion. Another voice, from a large Lutheran party in Germany, about their fellow Lutheran: Rudolf Bultmann is the arch-heretic of the century. More, from Norman Perrin, author of this book: Bultmann may well represent the end of traditional German Protestant theology.

How can one speak of "promise" in the career of such a problematic figure? Promise implies future. What future is there if he is the end of the line? These are reasonable questions, and Professor Perrin faces them both. He provides a succinct summary of Bultmann's position. (A remarkably consistent one it has been, by the way.) Implied criticism is blended with overt enthusiasm. But always there is one interest: in helping the reader to appraise Bultmann himself and then in helping him to transform that appraisal into the stuff of his own personal theology. Perrin is, in effect, telling us that among the giants of the century, Bultmann is one of the most difficult to avoid or evade. He deserves to be confronted and, if possible, understood. The possibility has been enriched by the pages which follow.

MARTIN E. MARTY

The University of Chicago

# I

# *Introduction*

For more than a hundred years German Protestant theology has dominated the scene so far as Protestantism is concerned, and it has heavily influenced Catholicism. It has been a very definite kind of theology, one that has stood consciously in a tradition which goes back to the great Reformers (especially, of course, Martin Luther), and yet at the same time has been eager to apply to itself the insights being developed in the fields of philosophy and of the natural and social sciences. Moreover, the men engaged in this theological endeavor have either been major scientific historians themselves, as for example Adolf Harnack was, or been very conscious of what was being done in the way of scientific historical study of the Bible or the history of Christian thought. In addition to this, they have always been conscious of the necessity for setting earliest Christianity in its immediate historical context of the comparative religious situation in the eastern Mediterranean in the first century A.D. and they have never hesitated to use the insights thereby developed in their own theological endeavors. A good example of this would be Albert Schweitzer's use of Jewish apocalypticism—in his day recently rediscovered—in his justly famous *Quest of the Historical Jesus*. Finally, this theology has always been characterized by a determination to speak theologically to the needs and situation of the particular cultural and historical circumstances in which the theologian himself was working: a Schleiermacher addressing the cultured despisers of religion at the turn of the nineteenth century, a Karl Barth[1] challenging the shattered society of Europe after the First World War. The endeavor to hold together these various factors—the strong sense of a theological tradition; the concern for philosophy, science and history; the willingness to consider the Christian faith historically, from the first century to the present; the passion for relevance to the immediate cultural-historical situation—has not been an easy one, but where it has been successful it has produced theology with a vitality and power unmatched anywhere else in the theological world. No other tradition in recent times can match a roll call which would include such names as David Friedrich Strauss and Ferdinand Christian Baur, Friedrich Schleiermacher and Albrecht Ritschl, Adolf Harnack and Albert Schweitzer, Karl Barth and Rudolf Bultmann.

Rudolf Bultmann is very much a part of this tradition; indeed, it may well be that in him this tradition reaches a climax—and perhaps also a period. Certainly he has all the characteristics to which we have referred. He is very much in the Lutheran tradition—however much some of his fellow Lutherans may deny it! He is very conscious indeed of the existentialist philosophy of Martin Heidegger and of the world view of modern science. He is both a major scientific historian (of the New Testament) and a very considerable philosopher of history. His program for demythologizing springs from a passionate concern to speak theologically to a generation he believes to be alienated by conventional Christian terminology. All in all, he is characteristic of the tradition from which he comes; he is one of its most recent representatives and one of its greatest. It is also possible that he may be the last of his line, for the question "Is Bultmann the last great German Protestant theologian?" is a very real one. Certainly the attempts so far made to challenge his position have involved abandoning one or another of the major characteristics of the theological tradition we have described above. That does not mean that this should not be done, for no tradition is sacrosanct, but it would mean that we were at the end of one era and the beginning of another and that

Bultmann would become what we have said he may well be: the climax and period of the tradition in which he stands.

Be that as it may, there can be no question but that Bultmann is the most influential German theologian today. Certainly this is the case so far as America is concerned; no other German can match him for impact upon the American theological scene. Moreover, it is a tribute to him that his impact has not been simply that of making converts to his theological position, although this has happened, but, rather, that his position has been the starting point for others. "Bultmann's brilliant and daring theological proposals have become the focus for much of the most creative theological work of our time," says John B. Cobb, Jr.,[2] one of the leaders of the younger generation of American theologians—and not himself a Bultmannian.

Perhaps the most remarkable thing about the whole business is that Bultmann is not professionally either a theologian or a philosopher of religion, but a New Testament scholar.[3] In his doctoral dissertation he concerned himself with a technical comparison of the preaching style of the apostle Paul with the diatribe of Hellenistic moral philosophy, and the subsequent research he carried out to qualify himself for an academic post in a German university was on the exegetical method of Theodore of Mopsuestia. (This is almost certainly the only thing he ever wrote which was never published.) His whole academic life has been spent as a Professor of New Testament studies and the next work of systematic theology he writes will be the first. As a New Testament scholar he is a towering figure, his achievements in his chosen field of specialization being equal to any and second to none.[4] But he is also and at the same time a major theologian, and why this should be the case requires a word of explanation.

All through his career Bultmann has been concerned to interpret the New Testament historically, to determine what it *said.* He has devoted himself to the task of understanding what a given New Testament author would have meant by the words he used and how the readers for whom he wrote would have understood him. At the same time he has been concerned to interpret the New Testament existentially, to determine what it *says* today to a man involved in living out his existence in the world. Furthermore, he is fully prepared to accept the theological position of major New Testament figures as normative, as giving expression to a Christian faith which is valid today. In this last connection he becomes at one and the same time a historical scholar and a theologian. He regards certain documents in the New Testament, especially the genuine Epistles of Paul[5] and the Gospel and Epistles of John[6] as giving expression to an understanding of the nature of Christian faith which is, or should be, normative for Christians in any age. Hence, as a historian he seeks to understand it and then as a theologian to express it in terms that will be real today. Theology is for him something that is ever changing in the sense that the theological task—"the task which consists of unfolding that understanding of God, and hence of the world and man, which arises from faith"[7] —needs to be carried out anew in every age, but at the same time it remains the same, since the essential nature of Christian faith remains the same; that is, the faith which is expressed by Paul and John is normative. The task is then to understand what they say in their language in order that we may say it in ours.

We should perhaps pause here for a moment to attempt to avoid confusion by pointing out that there are involved here two different ways of approaching the New Testament texts. The first is that of existential interpretation, which is concerned to approach the texts in such a way that they may become the word of God addressed to a man living out his existence in the world. This we mentioned only briefly above because we shall deal with it in some detail in Chapter VII. The mention here was simply for the sake of completeness. The second is that of seeking a normative expression of the nature of Christian faith, which will guide the theologian in his particular theological task. This we mentioned at some length above because it explains how Bultmann, a New Testament scholar, has become a major theologian. In expressing for his historical circumstances, for his day and age, the Christian faith which he finds in the Epistles of Paul and the Gospel and Epistles of John, he has developed the theological position which has made him the major force he is in the theological world. The fact that his theological position is a conscious attempt to unfold for his day the faith he finds in Paul and John explains another feature of his work to which we shall constantly be calling attention: the way in which he so readily moves backward and forward between his historical exegesis of Paul and John and his expression of his own theological position.

# II

# Life, Times and Work of Rudolf Bultmann

Rudolf Bultmann is a son and grandson of the pastorate. His father was a Lutheran pastor and his grandfather a missionary. There is no evidence that he ever considered any other vocation than that of the service of the church, nor that his conception of that service was ever anything other than that of an academic theologian. As a boy in high school *(Gymnasium)* he was already studying religion and at the age of nineteen he became a theological student at the University of Tübingen.[1] From that moment forward his career followed the path of the successful German academician. Born in 1884, he completed his qualifying studies in 1912 and was appointed a lecturer in New Testament at the University of Marburg in that same year. In quick succession he was appointed an Assistant Professor at Breslau (1916), Professor at Giessen (1920), and Professor at Marburg (1921), where he remained until his retirement (1951) and where he still lives.

A word about the significance of those dates is in order. His career as a student ran from 1903 to 1912, which means that his formative years were spent in the atmosphere of religious and cultural optimism that dominated Europe before the First World War. In theology this was the era of liberalism, of optimism about man and of a belief in the inevitability of spiritual and moral progress toward the establishment of the Kingdom of God on earth. At the same time the political forces that were to plunge Europe into war in 1914 were at work in the land, and in the field of theology prophetic voices, for example, that of Albert Schweitzer, were challenging the prevailing liberal consensus.

Two of Bultmann's own teachers should perhaps be mentioned because they represent particular influences which persist in his own thinking: Johannes Weiss and Wilhelm Herrmann. Weiss was his *Doktorvater*[2] and he constantly quotes Herrmann. Weiss was a member of the "history of religions school," a group of scholars who set themselves the particular task of studying earliest Christianity in its context among the religions of the eastern Mediterranean in the Hellenistic age. Weiss himself was concerned to study the message of Jesus in light of what the key phrase "Kingdom of God" would have meant to Jesus and his hearers, and he revolutionized theological scholarship[3] by demonstrating that the reference would be to God irrupting into history as an overpowering divine storm to bring to a violent end the world and its history and to create a new and radically different world and history. This was in very sharp contrast to the idea generally held before Weiss that the reference was to a world being gradually transformed by love as men accepted the rule of God in their hearts. In consequence of Weiss' influence, Bultmann consistently speaks of the Reign of God rather than the Kingdom of God so as to stress the fact that the reference is to God and to something that he does, and Bultmann always interprets the message of Jesus as "controlled by an imminent expectation of the Reign of God."[4] In his career as a New Testament scholar, Bultmann himself became the most distinguished latter-day representative of the "history of religions school" and his book *Primitive Christianity in Its Contemporary Setting* is a perfect example of the kind of work that school set out to do.

Herrmann was a systematic theologian who helped to shape much of the contemporary theological scene in that he profoundly influenced both Barth and Bultmann.[5] He counted himself not a liberal because he felt that liberalism was more concerned with man than with God. At the same time he could not move in the direction of Christian ortho-doxy because he held that to accept a creed was to stifle the individual's own particular search for certainty in religious matters. This individual search for religious certainty was his ruling concern, and he believed that it was to be found in the inner life of Jesus as this is presented in the Scriptures. Through the Scriptures men are confronted by God as he makes himself known through the reality of the inner life of Jesus, and in this experience of confrontation with God men find that individual certainty which is faith and which trans-forms their lives. Thereafter, men have the certainty that their lives are transformed and, although they cannot speak directly of God, they can speak of their lives transformed by him. There is much here to which Bultmann is directly in-debted. As James D. Smart puts it: "When we hear Herr Herrmann say, 'God reveals himself to us only in the inner transformation which we experience . . . . The religious man is certain that God has spoken to him, but what he can say of the event always takes the form of a statement concerning his transformed life . . . since religion is the transition from what only seems to be life to what is truly life,' we seem to be hearing the voice of Bultmann."[6]

As a young professor Bultmann lived through the hysteria which led to the First World War, that war itself, and its catastrophic social and cultural consequences for Germany. In theology the new voice was that of Karl Barth whose *Commentary on Romans* was first published in 1919. This marks the beginning of dialectical theology, or neo-orthodoxy, as it is sometimes called, a theology which chal-lenged men to listen to the word of God in a world that lay in ruins, and Bultmann himself was most responsive to this challenge. For a number of years he and Barth were regarded as belonging together among the dialectical theologians.

Bultmann was in Marburg from 1921 on. In 1921 his *History of the Synoptic Tradition* first appeared and this epoch-making book, which we shall describe in more detail below, fully established him as a major force in the field of

New Testament scholarship. It also demonstrated that the material found in the Synoptic Gospels (Matthew, Mark and Luke) was of such a nature as to raise serious questions about the liberal theological convictions that the historical Jesus could be known through the Gospels and that he was, or should be, the central concern of Christian faith. Thus, by 1922 Bultmann, who counted liberal theology as his own immediate theological heritage, had reasons to challenge this theological standpoint. In addition to the social and political catastrophe, the prophetic voices he would have heard as a student had led to this—so had Karl Barth's *Commentary on Romans*—and now there was in addition the results of his own technical work on the Synoptic tradition. Moreover, in 1922 he was thirty-eight years of age and so approaching the full maturity of his own mind. All in all, the stage was set for a fundamental thinking through of his theological position, and it was precisely at this time that he met the man who was to influence him more than any other: the German existentialist philosopher, Martin Heidegger. Heidegger taught philosophy at the University of Marburg from 1922 to 1928 and it was during this time that he published the book for which he is best known, *Sein und Zeit (Being and Time)*. Bultmann was constantly in conversation with him and all through his subsequent theological work was to be consciously indebted to him.

It was in the period between 1922 and 1928 that Bultmann hammered out the details of his own particular way of interpreting the New Testament and came to develop his own distinctive theological position. We shall be concerned with these things through the remainder of this book and with the particulars of Heidegger's influence, especially in Chapter III. At the moment all we need to say is that at this time the essays and books began to appear which are characteristic of what today could be called the Bultmannian theology: "Die liberale Theologie und die jüngste theologische Bewegung" ("Liberal Theology and the Most Recent Theological Movement"—the reference is to the dialectical theology of Karl

Barth) in 1926; "The Concept of Revelation in the New Testament" in 1929; and "The Historicity of Man and Faith" in 1930. From this point forward there are no significant changes in Bultmann's theological position; all the work he does from here on is a consequence of the fundamental thinking through of the problems and issues he must have done in the 1920s.

There is perhaps one more thing that needs to be said about Bultmann, and it is something which I approach with real reluctance since I have never met Professor Bultmann personally and hence can only speculate. But the matter is of sufficient importance in an American context for even speculation to be justifiable. From the beginning of his life to the present, Bultmann has devoted himself totally to the academic study of the New Testament and of theology. Although he has been closely touched by the historical circumstances under which he has lived—he lost one brother in the First World War and a second in a concentration camp during the Hitler regime—he has never "directly and actively participated in political affairs."[7] In other words, he has always sought to serve the cause of truth as he saw it as an academic theologian rather than lay his profession aside for a while to serve temporarily in some other way. It is therefore characteristic of him that his resistance to Hitler took the form of refusing to modify his lectures to suit the Nazi ideology[8] and of supporting the Confessional Church. But even in this latter the spirit of the academic theologian shines through: "Finally, I must mention that my work during the Hitler regime was fructified by the struggle of the church. I have belonged to the Confessing Church since its founding in 1934, and . . . [I] have endeavored to see that in it also free scientific work retained its proper place in face of reactionary tendencies."[9]

A survey of some of the more important essays and books written by Bultmann is presented in the Bibliography (see p. 106), concentrating first upon works of a general theological interest and then upon the more technical work in New Testament studies. By any rough count, Bultmann has writ-

16

ten some ten books, more than one hundred and fifty articles and review articles and more than one hundred and seventy book reviews—truly a prodigious output.

# III

# *Theology, Faith, and Authentic Existence*

During the late 1920s Bultmann became known—indeed he deliberately made himself known—as one who was using the insights of his philosopher colleague and friend, Martin Heidegger, in the service of theology. Heidegger analyzed human existence as an existentialist philosopher and he published his work in a famous book, *Sein und Zeit (Being and Time)* in 1926. As previously mentioned, Bultmann became convinced, in discussion with Heidegger, that this particular analysis of human existence corresponded at many important points to that understanding of the nature of human existence implied in the New Testament and that, further, it could be used in the development of a Christian theology. Because of the ever-present link in Bultmann's thinking between the New Testament and his own theology, these two things were one and the same for him, the two sides of the one coin.

We are here concerned, then, with Bultmann's use of the categories developed by Heidegger in the service of his theology, the use he makes of them in seeking to understand human existence prior to faith and in faith, and we may perhaps best begin by pointing out that for Bultmann the task of theology is precisely that of developing an understanding of human existence in faith. In 1924, under the influence of the then new dialectical theology of Karl Barth, Bultmann roundly claimed: "The central concern of theology is God and the complaint against liberal theology is that it has not been concerned with God but with man."[1] In 1930, on the other hand, he can say: ". . . it is . . . man that is the object of theology"![2] When we have learned to resolve this apparent paradox we shall have come closer to understanding Bultmann.

For Bultmann, God is the wholly other, the one who radically transcends the world. It has been well said by John B. Cobb, Jr., that "if Bultmann's thought is to be accurately grasped, one must begin with his understanding of the relation between God and the world."[3] For the moment we are concerned with the fact that God does so radically transcend the world, as Bultmann conceives the matter, that he can never be the object of human thought. Human thought can never grasp God at all because human thought is limited to objects within the world, within history, within the grasp of humanity. So, if God were to become something of which the mind of a man could conceive, then he would cease to be God. But what then can a theologian do? How can God be the central concern of theology if he is beyond the range of the human mind?

Let us approach the answer to this question by asking another. If God cannot be an object to human thought, what can a man think about? The answer would be that, among many other things, he can think about human existence in the world. He can think of man, of his hopes and fears, of his dreams and doubts, of his past and future. Insofar as he does this carefully and systematically he is a philosopher, and the task of philosophy is to arrive at an understanding of human existence in the world. Alexander Pope's famous line, "The proper study of mankind is man," could certainly have been paraphrased by Bultmann as, "The proper object for human thought is human existence," and he would mean, necessarily and specifically, "human existence in the world." Nevertheless, Bultmann does believe in God. While God cannot be the object of human thought, he can be known to human existence as the one who determines that existence. Although God radically transcends the world he determines human existence in the world. This is a paradox and it is one of several paradoxes which Bultmann unashamedly maintains as essential to Christian theology.

Let us come at this matter in another way. Bultmann has a lively horror of "talking about" the fundamentals of human existence because this necessarily objectifies what is being talked about and gives the speaker a viewpoint outside it. The relationship between the speaker and that of which he speaks becomes a subject-object relationship and however proper this relationship may be in the natural sciences, in the case of the fundamentals of human existence—God, for example, or love—it is improper, for the necessary intimacy of the relationship is thereby broken:

> It makes just as little sense to talk about God as it does to talk about love. In fact it is impossible to talk *about* love unless the talking about love be itself an act of love. All other talking about love is no speech of love, for it takes a position outside of love . . . . [Love] comes into being only as a condition of life itself; it only *is* in that I love or am loved, not as something secondary or derived.[4]

One cannot talk about love and thereby know love; one can only love and be loved. Still less can one talk about God; one can, however, encounter God in the immediacy and intimacy of one's personal existence.

This concept of the possibility of "encounter" with God is the crux of this matter for Bultmann, and he returns to it again and again. In this moment of encounter one knows God as the Lord of one's existence, and from that moment one can talk about God because one can now talk about one's existence as determined by him. In 1925 we find Bultmann saying:

> Only when one knows himself to be addressed by God in his own life does it make sense to speak of God as the lord of reality . . . . [If we are not addressed by God] we cannot talk about our existence because we cannot talk about God; and we cannot talk about God because we cannot talk about our existence. We could only do one if we could do the other. . . . . In any case a talking about God, if it were possible, would have to be at the same time a talking about us.

Thus it remains true: if it is asked how it is possible to speak of God, then it must be answered, only by speaking of us.[5]

In 1963 he says:

Only the idea of God which can find, which can seek and find, *the unconditional in the conditional,* the beyond in the here, the transcendent in the present at hand, as possibility of encounter, is possible for modern man.

It then remains to keep oneself open at any time for *the encounter with God in the world, in time.* It is not the acknowledgement of an image of God, be it ever so correct, that is real faith in God; rather it is the readiness for the eternal to encounter us at any time in the present—at any time in the varying situations of our life. Readiness consists in openness in allowing something really to encounter us that does not leave the I alone, the I that is encapsulated in its purposes and plans, but the encounter with which is designed to transform us, to make us new selves.[6]

God, then, cannot be known as the one who determines human existence by philosophy but only by Christian faith. Philosophy can analyze human existence in its actuality and potentiality but it cannot analyze it as determined by God. Only faith can do that, for only faith can know God as the one who determines human existence. Since the man of faith is still a man, he cannot, even as a man of faith, know God as the object of his thought; he can only know God as the determinant of his existence. He cannot think of God except in these terms. Hence, when he becomes a theologian, the central concern of his theology is God as the one who determines his human existence in the world; the direct object of his thought is his human existence in the world as determined by God.

Now we are in a position to understand the various statements which Bultmann makes about theology. The central concern of theology is God, not man, but it is God known as determining human existence in the world. If we complete the sentence of which we quoted a part above, it reads: "However, the object of an existential analysis of man is man; and it is likewise man that is the object of theology."

21

This is now clear; the existential analysis of man is concerned with human existence in the world and so is theology. Another favorite statement of Bultmann's concerning theology is that it is the careful and systematic self-interpretation of faith or that it is the unfolding of faith's understanding of God, the world and man.[7] Now we can see this also because human existence as determined by God can be known only to faith; hence, theology can be carried on only by the man of faith, just as love can be talked about only as an act of love.

Given these convictions about theology, human existence, and faith, it is easy to see why Martin Heidegger became so important to Bultmann. He became important to him because he offered him precisely that analysis of human existence in the world which Bultmann found he could take up and use in his theological concern for human existence as determined by God. It is now necessary, therefore, for us to say something of Heidegger's analysis of human existence as it is taken up and used by Bultmann.[8]

Heidegger's term for man is *Dasein,* literally "being-there," and this is important, for it indicates two things about the way in which Heidegger conceives of man: he is "being," that is, he is not a closed and complete entity but a continually existing, developing, changing one; and he is "being-there," he is existing, developing, changing in the actual concrete, historical world. As "being," man is continually having to respond, to decide, to act, to "be" as a given individual in the world of reality, of time and change and circumstances. At the same time, this individual is not pure self with unlimited possibilities for decision and action; he is man in the world, his decisions and actions are determined by the possibilities presented in his personal circumstances. He lives in an actual place, within the concrete set of circumstances at a given moment in history, and there is no escaping the place, the circumstances or the history. He is "being-there" and his "being-there" is "being-in-the-world." At the same time, man is not an object among other objects in the world; he is a man and not a tree, a flower or bird. As a man he has an ultimate control over his own existence because he can determine it by the decisions he makes. He can only determine it within the limited possibilities presented to him by the actuality of his own personal and historical circumstances, but within those limits his decisions are all-important as to the nature of his existence in the world.

At this point we should perhaps take the occasion to say that neither Heidegger nor Bultmann is concerned only with the nature of existence in the world as this is determined by the level of one's income, by the nature of one's professional occupation, or by the color of one's skin. What concerns the existentialist philosopher or theologian is also the nature of one's existence as this is revealed in the moment when one faces the ultimate questions of life; the inevitability of death, for example, or the constant frustration of any attempt to achieve the good in the world of men. This kind of existentialism comes alive, not only in the decision as to whether or not to go on to graduate school after college, or to marry the perfectly charming daughter of a friend of the family—important though these decisions are in the long run—but also in the decisions as to where to go after Auschwitz or what to do in a country which sees in short order the assassinations of John F. Kennedy, Martin Luther King, Jr., and Robert F. Kennedy. We are concerned here with every possible level of decision: the decisions made every day in response to the necessities of historical existence in the world and the decisions made but once or twice in a lifetime in response to the ultimate challenges that the world can pose.

In the analysis of human existence carried out by Heidegger in the early 1920s, the problems presented by human existence in the world were not presented in terms of specific moral outrages, since the concern of the philosopher was not with the concrete instance, but with the general theme. So Heidegger concerns himself with two things which are threats to all human existence: care and death.

By "care" Heidegger means to call attention to an essential characteristic of human existence. Man as man exists in the

23

constant necessity for decision; he is, so to speak, what he will become tomorrow because of the decisions he will make today. There is no escaping these decisions, because simply to drift is also a decision which will determine what one will be tomorrow. Further, man has always to contend with the concrete immediacies of the life he lives in the world; he must constantly contend with the brute facts of life in the world, with the search for food, shelter, companionship, safety from enmity and the like. He is thrown into a concrete historical situation and he must of necessity contend with the facts of life presented to him by that situation. Finally, he must constantly wrestle with the temptation to abandon himself to the concrete historical circumstances with which he must be constantly concerned. Man as a being in the world is forever in danger of choosing that world as his home and surrendering himself to it. "These three structures of man—being ahead of himself, being already in the world, being concerned with the world as his home—together constitute care."[9]

The nature of man as "being-there" as "being-in-the-world" necessarily involves him in "care," which is a threat to his existence; however, the ultimate threat is not care but death. "Death is the end of man as 'being-there' as 'being-in-the-world.' "[10] Death is the end of being, for in death one simply ceases to be; at the same time, death is the one inescapable possibility of human existence. The being of man is necessarily a "being-unto-death." Man constantly seeks to escape from the realization of the inevitability of death. He uses circumlocutions to avoid speaking of it directly; he regards it as the ultimate indecency, the very thought of which is to be avoided until the last possibile moment and the fact of which is to be fought with all resources at one's disposal. Life itself is a constant flight from death.

The nature of life in the world then is such that it is characterized by care and the threat of death, and everyday existence in the world is bedeviled by care and shot through and through with the necessity to flee from death. This everyday existence is a fallen existence, an inauthentic exist-

24

ence. So long as a man exists under the torment of care and the necessity to flee from the threat of death, his existence can never achieve its true potential and it can never become authentic existence.

It is as we come to this contrast between inauthentic and authentic existence that we reach the heart of the matter so far as Bultmann's indebtedness to Heidegger is concerned. Heidegger describes man as "being-in-the-world" confronted by the potentiality of authentic existence, but because of the care which besets him and the flight from death which characterizes him he does not in fact achieve that potential. However, such an achievement is in principle possible. As Bultmann expresses his understanding of Heidegger in the essay "The Historicity of Man and Faith," for Heidegger man *is* free to choose his possibility of existing authentically. That choice is possible for him in that moment when he is confronted by death and, finding himself shattered by the inevitable prospect, resolves to accept his being-there in the world bounded by death. Bultmann calls this "a resolution of despair." Our immediate concern is with the nature of the choice, with what it is that man actually does in that moment of choice. The word used by Heidegger is actually *Entschlossenheit* which may be translated "resolve" or "decision." What happens in the moment of choice is that man chooses resolutely to accept the certainty of death and the nothingness of human existence. In doing this he achieves authentic existence because he now has no necessity to delude himself about his being-in-the-world. We may say that he comes to know that it is bounded by death and limited by the facts of life, and in the resolve to accept this he finds the power to go through with it. Authentic existence is possible on the basis of this ultimate decision. Being confronted by the inevitability of death, man has to resolve to accept it and out of this resolve find the courage to face the care of being-in-the-world.[11] Being-in-the-world can include the possibility of authentic existence as well as the reality of inauthentic existence.

The central concepts in Heidegger's analysis of human existence for Bultmann are those of man as "being-there" and as "being-in-the-world," of human existence as having the potentiality for becoming authentic, and of the achievement of authentic existence coming as the result of a resolute decision to accept the inevitability of death and in this acceptance to find the courage to face the "care" which human existence necessarily involves. What Bultmann does in effect is, first, to accept the analysis of human existence as having the potential of becoming authentic and at this point to introduce the idea of God as the one who determines human existence—authentic existence is possible only when God makes it so. Second, he accepts the idea of resolute decision on the part of a man as that which makes the transition from inauthentic to authentic existence, and here he introduces the concept of this decision being made in response to that encounter with God which makes it possible.

Bultmann's thinking on these points is spread throughout his writings. Particular examples would be the essay, "The Historicity of Man and Faith," in *Existence and Faith*; the sections on Paul and John in his *Theology of the New Testament*; his initial essay on demythologizing and subsequent responses to his critics, now in *Kerygma and Myth,* and *Jesus Christ and Mythology*. The very range of titles here is significant. Bultmann can use this philosophical analysis of human existence in his own theology because for him, as we have seen, theology is thinking about human existence in faith. He can use it in his *Theology of the New Testament* because he finds that it illuminates the understanding of human existence implicit there, especially in the Epistles of Paul and the Gospel and Epistles of John. He can use it, finally, in his demythologizing program because that is essentially an interpretation of biblical myths into these very categories which he had worked out in dialogue with Heidegger. We shall concentrate our attention on some of the things he says in *Jesus Christ and Mythology*, since this is a mature statement of his position in the light of a great deal of discussion and because it is a statement originally made in English and designed for an American audience.

Existentialist philosophy shows the individual man, the "me," what it means to exist. It shows him this because it teaches him to distinguish between the being of man as "existing" and the being of things in the world which do not "exist" but are only "extant." Only man can "exist" because only man is a historical being whose existence is characterized by the responsibility of decision in concrete historical circumstances. Only man can have a history and every man has his own history. "Always his present comes out of his past and leads into his future. He realizes his existence if he is aware that each 'now' is the moment of free decision. . . . No one can take another's place, since every man must die his own death. In his loneliness every man realizes his existence."[12]

Philosophical analysis, therefore, helps us to understand ourselves in that it shows us what existence in the abstract means. But we truly understand ourselves as we come to grips with the existential realities of our personal existence. "Existential, personal self-understanding does not say what existence means in the abstract, but points to my life as a concrete person in the here and now. It is an act of understanding in which my very self and the relationships in which I am involved are understood together."[13]

Here we must pause for a moment to make two points about the terms which Bultmann uses in his discussion of these matters. The first is that he distinguishes between *das Existential* and *das Existentielle.* In English there is now a convention to render the former "existentialist" and the latter "existential." The distinction is between existentialist as "appertaining to existentialist philosophy" and existential as "appertaining to the concrete reality of a personal existence." In the discussion which we reported immediately above, when Bultmann says that philosophical analysis helps us to understand existence in the abstract, he is talking about the existentialist understanding of existence (*das Existential*), but when he speaks of our truly understanding ourselves by coming to grips with the realities of our personal existence, he has in mind an existential understanding of existence (*das Existentielle*).

The second point we must make about terminology is that there is a tendency to move between two terms which refer to the same thing: "understanding of existence" and "self-understanding." In the abstract analysis of existentialist philosophy it is natural to talk about "understanding of existence" and to consider carefully the understanding of existence as either inauthentic or authentic. But when we come to the concrete realities of our own personal existence it is equally natural to drop "my understanding of my existence" and to talk about "my self-understanding." What is "understanding of existence" in a discussion of the existentialist analysis of human existence can become "self-understanding" in a discussion of the existential reality of existence. This tendency to say "self-understanding" when one means "the self's understanding of its own existence in concrete historical and existential terms" has to be kept in mind because if it is not kept in mind, then self-understanding can be confused with self-consciousness.

Each person has an existential self-understanding, an understanding of his own existence in the world, and this understanding develops and changes by reason of "situations of encounter." "This personal self-understanding is called into question in every situation of encounter. As my life goes on, my self-understanding may prove inadequate or it may become clearer or deeper as the result of further experiences and encounters." Especially significant is the encounter with love. "Entering into decisive encounters I may achieve a totally new self-understanding as a result of the love which is bestowed upon me when, for example, I marry or make a new friend."[14]

We have now become acquainted with the first two features of Bultmann's existentialist theology: "self-understanding" and "encounter." Self-understanding is the self's understanding of its existential, concrete, actual existence in the world in accordance with the possibilities provided for this understand-

28

ing by the existentialist analysis of human existence in the world. Encounter is that event in which the self is confronted by the necessity for decision, the necessity for a decision which will affect one's self-understanding. For self-understanding is achieved, lost, modified or developed by the decisions which are forced upon one by those encounters which are a necessary part of being-in-the-world. To use our own terms, these encounters can be brutal—Auschwitz, the assassinations in America—or they can be gentle—love of a mother, the making of a friend. They can be from the past—the challenge of the self-understanding revealed in the teaching of Jesus or the deeds and words of Abraham Lincoln—or they can come from the future—the necessity of providing for retirement or of facing loneliness after the loss of a loved one. The one thing they all have in common is that necessity for decision which will further shape that self-understanding which makes a man what he is in his own personal, existential being-in-the-world.

A third feature of the Bultmannian existentialism is his stress on the fact that self-understanding always has consequences in terms of the self's attitudes and actions. "Personal self-understanding dominates or exercises a powerful influence upon all our sorrows and cares, ambitions, joys and anxieties . . . . Even a little child unconsciously manifests such self-understanding in so far as he realizes that he is a child and that he therefore stands in a special relationship to his parents. His self-understanding *expresses itself in his love, trust, feeling of security, thankfulness, etc.*"[15] This necessary relationship between self-understanding and the attitudes and actions in which that self-understanding expresses itself is very important because it is the key to understanding the role and place of ethics in Bultmann's theology.

It is important to note that up to this point Bultmann is concerned with what can be called "inauthentic existence," or "human existence apart from faith,"[16] or "self-understanding," as distinct from the "new self-understanding," the "self-understanding of faith." It is Bultmann's claim that this existence is necessarily inauthentic and can never be anything else, that the existentialist analysis of human existence reveals authentic existence to be a possibility in principle (ontological possibility), but the experience of being-in-the-world reveals that it is not a possibility in fact (ontic possibility). At this point Bultmann clearly reveals himself as a Lutheran theologian and as an interpreter of the New Testament who stands in the Lutheran tradition. This claim that authentic existence is not possible in fact in the world apart from faith is explicitly a theological claim, and its ultimate justification is the New Testament as it is understood in the Lutheran tradition. Bultmann never tries to hide this; on the contrary, he explicitly avows it over and over again. Let us look at two quotations from his 1930 essay, "The Historicity of Man and Faith." In the first of them he is defending his claim that "theology as a science can make fruitful use of the philosophical analysis of human existence" and he is concerned in particular with the fruitfulness of the distinction between an ontological possibility and an ontic possibility—the distinction between the possibility in principle and the possibility in fact with which we are now familiar. He illustrates this distinction in terms of a central affirmation of faith.

> Indeed, when faith affirms, for example, that it is impossible for man to be righteous before God through his works, that he has therefore necessarily missed the possibility of laying hold of his authenticity in the decision that essentially belongs to his existence, the impossibility that is meant is an ontic or *existentiell* one. And to speak of such a impossibility is only possible and meaningful if one can speak ontologically or existentially about the possibility of "righteousness." To say of an animal that it is impossible for it to be rightwised by the works of the law is clearly meaningless because righteousness is not an ontological possibility for it.[17]

The concern of the preceding paragraph is to argue that an ontic possibility—a possibility in fact—can be found only where an ontological possibility—a possibility in principle—already exists. Our concern is not with this but with the affirmation of faith chosen as the example. It is the more telling since it is simply assumed that faith can and does

30

affirm this, that man can never achieve authentic existence—"he has necessarily missed the possibility of laying hold of his authenticity"—and that the basis for this affirmation is a theological one—if a man could achieve authentic existence then this would be justification by works, a possibility fundamentally denied by the New Testament and the Lutheran theological tradition.

The second quotation concerns the possibility of the transition to authentic existence held out by Heidegger's philosophy. Bultmann interprets Heidegger on this point as claiming that a man must be confronted by the inevitability of death, be shattered by this, and then resolve simply to accept his being-there as a being-in-the-world. He is then concerned to deny that this is a true transition to authentic existence because it is a resolution of despair and does nothing about the problem of sin. Our concern here is simply to call attention to the central role played here by the Christian theological affirmation that authentic existence is Christian freedom, that is, freedom from sin. Again, this is not debated; it is simply affirmed as a claim of faith.

> Furthermore, the claim of the man of faith that he alone is free does not compete with the ontological exhibition of man's freedom for his possibility of existing authentically; for Christian freedom is freedom from sin. Therefore, it is the judgment of faith that wherever the freedom of man that is exhibited ontologically realizes itself ontically without doing so in faith and love, it is not freedom. Similarly, it claims that wherever resolution realizes itself ontically in that an actual man, being shattered by death, lets himself be thrown back upon his being-there and resolves in the situation and thus for himself, it is really a *resolution of despair.*[18]

So we can see that Bultmann is justified in his claim that his scientific theology is "making use" of the existential analysis of human existence. At the crucial point of the transition to authentic existence he simply abandons it to make an "affirmation of faith," and his ultimate justification for this is simply and always an appeal to the New Testament as he interprets it, standing as he does in the Lutheran theological tradition. It is for this reason that a philosopher such as Karl Jaspers tends to regard him as an obscurantist whereas his fellow Lutheran theologians tend to regard him as a radical!

The indebtedness of Bultmann to the New Testament and to the Lutheran theological tradition is nowhere clearer than in his description of "authentic existence" or the "self-understanding" of faith as he understands it. The following paragraph from *Jesus Christ and Mythology* is typical:

> Mutatis mutandis we may here apply the saying, "if we live by the Spirit, let us also walk by the Spirit" (Gal. 5:25). For indeed the saying is applicable to the self-understanding of faith, which is a response to our encounter with the word of God. In faith man understands himself anew. As Luther says in his interpretation of the Epistle to the Romans, "God going out from Himself brings it about that we go into ourselves; and making Himself known to us, He makes us known to ourselves." In faith man understands himself ever anew. This new self-understanding can be maintained only as a continual response to the word of God which proclaims His action in Jesus Christ. It is the same in ordinary human life. The new self-understanding which grows out of the encounter of man with man can be maintained only if the actual relation between man and man is maintained. "The kindness of God is new every morning"; yes, provided I perceive it anew every morning. For this is not a timeless truth, like a mathematical statement. I can speak of the kindness of God which is new every morning only if I myself am renewed every morning.[19]

For Bultmann, then, authentic existence is only ontically possible in faith, and faith itself is a response to an encounter with the word of God, and a major part of his indebtedness to existentialist philosophy is for the terms he uses to explain these theological affirmations.

Before we can go further into Bultmann's theology, there is a second set of terms he uses which needs some discussion. There terms are: *history*, the *historicity of man*, and *eschatology*, and we turn now to a discussion of them.

# IV
# *History, the Historicity of Man, and Eschatology*

Nothing is more difficult for the general reader to grasp than the varied uses of the word "history" that are to be found in Bultmann and in discussions of the Bultmannian theology. There are actually four different conceptions that need to be taken into account. Unfortunately it is not possible to list them entirely in English because the English language does not have enough nouns to cover them. German does, but only because the German language happens to have two different words for "history" and the theologians decided, quite arbitrarily, to give these words different meanings. The list then has to read: history as *Historie*; history as *Geschichte*; the historicity of man; eschatology. We shall now try to give some account of them and the role they play in Bultmann's thinking. As we do this we shall be in part covering ground that will already be familiar to a reader of our previous chapters and it is hoped that the repetition in a new context will help to clarify the difficulties which the reader may still be having in understanding what has been said.

## History as *Historie*

In the first place we have history in the sense of "what actually happened," in the sense of historical factuality. For this kind of history Bultmann would use the word *Historie* and cognate adjective *historisch*. So he would say, for example, "the historical (*historisch*) Jesus," meaning "Jesus as he actually was." This kind of history is subject to investigation by the historical sciences. If we want to know anything about this Jesus we have to turn to the scientific historians of the New Testament period, to Bultmann himself and his *Jesus and the Word*, or to his pupil Günther Bornkamm and his *Jesus of Nazareth*, and we shall find them using the kind of methodology that I described in *Rediscovering the Teaching of Jesus*. As we shall see later, it is one of Bultmann's major insights that this kind of historical knowledge cannot serve as the basis for faith; indeed, it is extremely characteristic of his theology that he tends to minimize the significance of this kind of history altogether. There are three reasons for this and they are all important.

1. The first problem is that this kind of knowledge is always ambiguous. We cannot be sure that some new discovery, or some new way of interpreting existing evidence, will not cause us drastically to revise what we previously accepted as firm historical knowledge. All practicing historians become aware of this and Bultmann, an extremely good practicing historian, is more aware of it than most. Indeed, one of the most spectacular incidents of it came during Bultmann's formative student days in connection with research into the life of Jesus. For a generation it had been held that Jesus actually was a prophetic reformer figure who by teaching and moral example had started a movement of spiritual and moral reform which was still growing and developing in the world. Then came the discovery of apocalyptic literature, and the work of Johannes Weiss (Bultmann's teacher) and perhaps still more Albert Schweitzer's *Quest of the Historical Jesus*—and all this changed. Jesus was now seen as a deluded apocalyptic fanaticist who expected God to bring the world to an end at harvest time in the year in which he was conducting his ministry. Today things have changed again and we have a still different view of Jesus "as he actually was." But that is the whole point: the picture of Jesus "as he actually was" has been forever changing since scientific life-of-Jesus research began. We may think today that our picture of him is the best that has yet been produced, and it certainly is

that, but still better ones will be produced tomorrow, and neither we nor the scholars of tommorrow can ever be sure that our picture will not have to change as suddenly and drastically as the liberal picture of the historical Jesus had to change under the impact of the discovery of the apocalyptic literature and the new interpretation of the evidence by Albert Schweitzer. So a faith built on the historical Jesus may look firm and secure today only to be revealed as extremely ambiguous tomorrow.

2. The second problem is that all history is relative and all historical knowledge can only be knowledge of things which belong in a category with other things. To a historian nothing is unique; it can only be that some things are more spectacular than other things which belong in the same general category. If something were to come along for which a historian had no general category he would simply pigeonhole it as "not yet historical knowledge" until he found other examples and could establish a category. If the historian is faced with, for example, the resurrection of Jesus from the dead as a unique event within human history, then he can only say either that it is not unique or that it is not an event within the human history with which he deals. This is an important point which all practicing historians recognize, and Bultmann very much so, but it must be emphasized that these historians do not thereby claim to be the arbiters of what has been, what is, or what can be—practicing historians are much more reluctant to say the things about their work that some theologians will say for them!—but it does mean that the significance of the kind of history which historians investigate is severely limited so far as Christian faith is concerned.

3. Third, and perhaps most important of all for Bultmann is the fact that not only are there no unique events in history, but also that history which historians investigate is a closed chain of cause and effect. Phenomena observable within history have sufficient causation within history, they are the consequences of things which themselves can be observed within history, and they can always be explained in terms of

things which themselves have a historical explanation. The idea of God as a force intervening in history as an effective cause is one which a historian simply cannot contemplate. The effective cause would have to be faith in God such as could be held to motivate Martin Luther, for example, and so become as effective cause within history. But then as an effective cause in history such faith is by no means unique. So far as the historian is concerned it is paralleled by the "faith" motivating such other men in history as Alexander the Great, or Napoleon Bonaparte. This is fully recognized by Bultmann: ". . . the modern study of history . . . does not take account of any intervention of God . . . in the course of history. Instead, the course of history is considered to be an unbroken whole, complete in itself, though differing from the course of nature because there are in history spiritual powers which influence the will of persons. Granted that not all historical events are determined by physical necessity and that persons are responsible for their actions, nevertheless nothing happens without rational motivation."[1]

For all that he has spent a lifetime investigating the historical origins of Christian faith, it can be seen that Bultmann is prepared to grant little significance for that faith to the results of his historical labors, and, if his three reasons hold up, then he is certainly justified in his attitude.

## History as *Geschichte*

The second of the conceptions linked to the word "history" is that of history in the sense of an event from the past living on in influence upon and significance for the future. The second of the two German words for history, *Geschicte,* is used to denote history in this sense. The distinction has become current in German theology largely under the influence of a book published in 1892 by Martin Kähler, *Der sogenannte historische Jesus und der geschichtliche, biblische Christus* (translated by C. E. Braaten as *The So-called Historical Jesus and the Historic, Biblical Christ).* In this book

Kähler distinguished between the *historische* Jesus, the historical Jesus—Jesus "as he actually was," Jesus as he may be known as a result of scientific historical investigation—and the *geschichtliche* Christ, the historic Christ—the Christ who is presented by the Gospels in narratives which interpret him in his significance for faith, the Christ who is at one and the same time a figure from the past and an influence in the present. Braaten's translation of Kähler's work uses the English adjective "historic" for the German adjective *geschichtlich* and "historical" for *historisch*, and this is now the convention in the English-language discussion of German theology. Unfortunately we have not yet been able to think of a noun to use in English so as to be able to distinguish history as *Geschichte* from history as *Historie*.

For all that this distinction may sound artificial, it is in fact very useful, for there is a real difference between an event in its quality of "that-ness," of "what-actually-happenedness" and an event as it lives on in subsequent narration, interpretation and influence. Every president of the United States of America, for example, is equally a historical person but very few of them can be as historic as is Abraham Lincoln. The reason for this is not so much that he was president in particularly demanding circumstances as it is that the quality of the man himself, as revealed in his response to the challenge of those circumstances, was such as to lift him out of the rut of the merely historical and to stamp his image indelibly on the future. There are, of course, any number of historical figures who also become historic, who live on in narration and interpretation to influence the future. Nor does the figure have to be noble or good; the Roman emperor Nero is also a historic figure.

One can understand why this kind of history, *Geschichte*, would be of great interest to an existentialist theologian such as Bultmann. As an existentialist he believes that a man achieves self-understanding precisely out of encounter with this kind of history. A historical event or person becomes a challenge to one's self-understanding only when it or he becomes historic. As simply people who lived in the past, neither Jesus nor Nero nor Abraham Lincoln means anything to an individual in the present at the level of his self-understanding. Their pictures may hang on the walls of a local museum, scholars may busy themselves in dusty archives establishing facts about them—or overturning previously "established facts" about them—and schoolchildren may be taken to see artifacts relating to their lives by the busload on a Saturday morning, but none of that means anything to a man struggling to establish meaningful existence in the world. It is only when the picture comes down from the wall to confront the man with a challenge to his existence in the present, only when a document comes out of the dusty archives where scholars debate its authenticity to become a living word spoken to that man's present—in other words when these things become historic—that they can play their pàrt in the struggle for meaningful existence, in the striving for self-understanding. So as a historian, Bultmann is very much interested in *Historie*, the historical, but as an existentialist, only in *Geschichte*, the historic. We shall find these distinctions very important when we come to discuss the significance of the historical Jesus in the Bultmannian theology.

## The Historicity of Man

In the preceding chapter we used two sets of terms to denote the existence of man in the world, both of which are used by Bultmann: existence, and the distinction between inauthentic and authentic existence; self-understanding, and the distinction between self-understanding and the new self-understanding, or between self-understanding and the self-understanding of faith. There is, however, a third set of terms which can be used and which Bultmann does occasionally use, for example, in his essay "The Historicity of Man and

Faith": historicity, and the distinction between inauthentic and authentic historicity.

An example will make clear the parallelism to which we are calling attention. In the course of the essay on the historicity of man and faith we find Bultmann saying "that man exists in both an 'authentic' and 'inauthentic' historicity" and then going on to make "the theological affirmation" that "man is only genuinely historical in faith and in love."[2] In other places Bultmann can make this same point by using either "existence" or "self-understanding." There is for him no distinction between historicity, existence or self-understanding; they can all be used equally well of "being-there's" "being-in-the-world," of a man's concrete life in time and space.

This use of historicity to describe man's existence in the world calls attention to the concrete nature of that existence. A man's existence is necessarily in part determined by the historical circumstances which surround him. If he is born a peasant in Asia he has one set of possibilities, middle-class Western European a second, a Negro in America a third, and so on. Moreover, at any given time the nature of a man's existence is in part determined by what he himself has done, or what has been done to him in his own past. Every decision he makes, every act he commits, every experience he undergoes has consequences for his future, and at any moment he can look back into his past and realize to what extent he has become what he is because of one or more of these things. Each man's existence in the world is what it is as a consequence of his own personal history. But there is more to it than this for each man is necessarily involved in the history of the time in which he lives. Events over which he has no control can seriously affect his personal existence. Wars, revolutions, technological advances, natural catastrophes, all the things which will eventually be reported as part of the history of the day and place in which he lives will affect him to a greater or less extent. Directly or indirectly the history of his time is also his history. So, a man becomes what he is partly because of factors over which he has no control, his historical circumstances, but still more because of the way he responds to the challenge of those circumstances.

To speak of the historicity of man is to call attention, then, to the fact that the decisions which a man makes, which ultimately determine the nature of his existence in the world, are decisions made in terms of the concrete realities which confront that man from day to day in his personal history. We called attention to the importance of this for Heidegger and Bultmann in Chapter III. But now there is a further point to be emphasized and it is that decisions can be made *only* as a consequence of an encounter which takes place at the level of a man's own personal history. In the discussion of history as *Geschichte* immediately above, we pointed out that the historical has to become the historic in order to confront a man with the necessity for decision. Now we want to express that another way by saying that the historical must become historic and encounter a man at the level of his historicity in order to confront him with the necessity for decision. The self-understanding of a man from the past has to take on meaning in terms of our personal historicity before it can challenge us; we cannot be challenged by a self-understanding which is totally foreign to us.

Bultmann's word for historicity, for example in the title of the essay, "The Historicity of Man and Faith," is *Geschichtlichkeit* and is from the same root as *Geschichte*. It is helpful to remember this because it calls attention to the essential connection for Bultmann between "history as *Geschichte*" and the "historicity of man" (*Geschichtlichkeit des Daseins*). The decisions which determine a man's existence in the world can only be made in response to something which confronts man at the level of his actual existence in the world. If we are to speak, therefore, of Jesus or God as significant for our existence, then we have to find a way of understanding how they encounter us at the level of our historicity, and that, as we shall see, is something which Bultmann is very concerned to do.

## Eschatology

Eschatology is technically "teaching concerning the end [of history]" from the Greek *eschaton* (end) and *logeia* (teaching), and in theological language it means "teaching concerning the last things"; that means, teaching concerning the final destiny of man in God's plan and design. In Judaism during the New Testament period there was a strong movement called "apocalyptic" (meaning "to uncover," "to reveal"), which concerned itself with uncovering or revealing God's plan for man, the Old Testament book of Daniel being the first major Jewish apocalyptic work. As this movement understood things, God was about to irrupt into human history to visit and redeem Israel, to bring human history to an end, and to establish the Kingdom of God. Apocalyptic eschatology therefore was concerned with a particular view of the "last things," namely, the intervention of God into history to destroy the old and establish the new. It was concerned with a particular view of the way in which God would act for the salvation of man. Bultmann has taken this apocalyptic eschatology very seriously indeed, in part because of his indebtedness to his teacher, Johannes Weiss, and in part because his own historical studies had shown him that it is highly characteristic of both Jesus and the early church. At the same time he refuses to take it literally, for already in the New Testament itself there is a movement away from it (partly away from it in Paul, wholly so in John), and in any case the ideas connected with it, such as that of a heavenly figure descending to earth on a cloud, are nonsense to modern technological man. What he does is to demythologize it, that is, to take away its mythical trappings of heavenly redeemers descending on clouds and so on, and to interpret it existentially, that is, to attempt to express its meaning in terms of man encountering God in the reality of his existence in the world.

The line of reasoning here might be described somewhat as follows. Eschatology is the teaching concerning the way in which God will put an end to the old world and establish a new. In the New Testament this is often expressed by such ideas as the coming of Jesus on a cloud as Son of man to judge the world. But the point is that God did not bring the world to an end in that way; he brought it to an end by making authentic existence possible. So eschatology is teaching concerning the way in which God has made authentic existence possible. Now God has made authentic existence possible by acting in Jesus Christ so "Jesus Christ is the eschatological event, the action of God by which God has set an end to the old world."[3]

The phrase "the eschatological event" is very important to Bultmann. It means "that event (or series of events) by means of which God brings to an end the old world of sin and establishes a new world of grace" and the reference would be to the kind of event described in chapter thirteen in Mark's Gospel, which itself is a characteristic piece of early Christian apocalyptic. For Bultmann, however, such an event never did take place, and never will take place, because actually the crucifixion of Jesus, the cross of Jesus, as proclaimed by the church fulfills this function. The action of God in the cross of Jesus and in the proclamation of that cross by the church is the eschatological event, the means by which "God has set an end to the old world." We shall come back to this essential feature of the Bultmannian theology later.

# V

# God, Jesus and History

In 1924 Bultmann published an essay. "Die liberale Theologie und die jüngste theologische Bewegung" ("Liberal Theology and the Newest Theological Movement"), [1] which is worth considering in some detail because it is an early statement of some of the basic elements in his theological position. He was now forty years of age, an established Professor at the University of Marburg, and he had begun the long association with Martin Heidegger (who had come to Marburg in 1922) which was to mean so much to him. Moreover, the "newest theological movement" was the dialectical theology of Karl Barth (in America often called "neo-orthodoxy") with which Bultmann was in sympathy and in light of which he was thinking out aspects of his own theology. All in all, therefore, this essay is a most significant one for our purpose.

The liberal theology with which the essay is concerned is typified by Adolf Harnack's *What is Christianity?* which has been reissued with an introduction written by Bultmann himself. The characteristics of this theology may be summarized somewhat as follows. Christian faith itself and the documents of that faith are to be subjected to rigorous and fearless historical critical examination. The central concern of Christian faith is the man Jesus bar Joseph from Nazareth, the historical Jesus, and when the true historical picture of this man is reconstructed from the Gospels he is found to be "a man who has rest and peace for his soul, and is able to give life and strength to others," a man who "lived in the continual consciousness of God's presence. . .[whose] food and drink was to do God's will." [2] The central concerns of Jesus were threefold. In the first place he proclaimed the Kingdom of God, by which is meant the rule of God within the individual human heart. Then, second, he taught the Fatherhood of God and the infinite value of the human soul. Third, he challenged men to the higher righteousness of the commandment of love. These must be the central concerns of Christianity today, for Christianity is essentially an acceptance of the religion *of* Jesus (in deliberate contrast to the religion *about* him). So Christians can learn to experience the light and joy of the acceptance of the rule of God in their hearts. They can come to value God as their father, to accept their role as his children and hence to know the infinite value of the human soul. As Jesus did, they must learn to combine religion and morality [3] by placing side by side the love of God and one's neighbors; the love of one's neighbor is the only practical proof on earth of that love of God. "We must steep ourselves again and again in the Beatitudes of the Sermon on the Mount," says Harnack, for "they contain [Jesus'] ethics and his religion, united at the root, and freed from all external and particularistic elements." [4]

Before turning to Bultmann's consideration of this kind of understanding of Christianity in light of the new dialectical theology, we might pause for a moment to point out a number of things that are in the background of Bultmann's essay and which need to be kept in mind if we are to read that essay in its true context. For one thing, Harnack's position was conceived in a period of cultural optimism and in this respect the Germany of the 1920s was very different from that of 1900. Then, further, Harnack was dependent upon a particular picture of the historical Jesus, a picture developed by what is now called "liberal life-of-Christ research." But this picture had already been challenged in four ways. (1) Albert Schweitzer in his famous book, *The Quest of the Historical Jesus,* had shown that a particular liberal picture of the historical Jesus was only too often a picture of the particular liberal historian's ideals. (2) Again Schweitzer had shown in the same book that Jesus was in fact far more concerned with eschatology than with morality, that his central concern was for the irruption of God into human history to shatter and remake that history. [5] (3) Bultmann himself in his *History of the Synoptic Tradition* had shown that the Gospel traditions are not of such a nature as to yield us the kind of biographical picture of Jesus that Harnack was presupposing, and hence to use such a picture as central to Christian faith is to be untrue to the nature of the Christian texts themselves. (4) Then, lastly, Martin Kähler in his book *The So-Called Historical Jesus and the Historic, Biblical Christ*[6] had challenged theology to recognize that Christian faith was not concerned with the historical Jesus as he may be reconstructed from the Gospel texts, but with Jesus Christ as presented in those texts. [7] This was to become a characteristic of dialectical theology.

Bearing these things in mind we are now in a position to turn to Bultmann's 1924 essay. The first point he makes which concerns us is that liberal theology failed to recognize that theology is concerned with *God,* for in practice liberal theology was more concerned with *man.* It was concerned with the man Jesus and his consciousness of God, his concern for morality, and so on, and it was concerned with how other men might echo that consciousness and concern. But God himself is lost in this, for God, truly conceived, means the radical negation of any possibilities that men may have and a true theology must therefore be a stumbling block, an offense, a scandal (Greek: *skandalon*) to men in the world.[8]

The use of "stumbling block" here is an early statement of one of the most prominent themes in Bultmann's theology. It is inspired by the use of *skandalon* in the New Testament, for example, I Corinthians 1:21-24: "For since, in the wisdom of God, the world did not know God through wisdom, it pleased God through the folly of what we preach to save those who believe. For Jews demand signs and Greeks seek wisdom, but we preach Christ crucified, a stumbling block [Greek: *skandalon*] to Jews and folly to Gentiles, but to those who are called, both Jews and Greeks, Christ the power of God and the wisdom of God." In his theology Bultmann has taken this kind of text very seriously indeed; in particular, he has derived four things from it. (1) God is not to be known by the normal methods of knowledge in the world (the "wisdom of the world"). (2) God is known through the Christian proclamation ("what we preach"; the Greek word is *kerygma,* a word which is also very prominent in Bultmann's writings). (3) The essential content of the Christian *kerygma* is the cross of Christ ("we preach Christ crucified"). (4) This is a *skandalon* to men ("to the Jews a stumbling block"), so also therefore will Christian theology be a scandal, offense, stumbling block, because theology is the careful and academic (*wissenschaftlich*) explication of the Christian proclamation (*kerygma*).

Returning to the essay, the next point to concern us is Bultmann's claim that one of the problems we have with liberal theology is that its central concern is with something within history, something revealed by historical investigation (the historical Jesus). We must be grateful for liberalism's concern for historical research and we ourselves must learn to practice historical criticism every bit as radically and fearlessly, but we must learn that there are limits here so far as Christian faith is concerned. In particular, historical research can only deal with entities which fit into contexts or categories broader than the entity itself, and a Christianity which is dependent upon this kind of history (history as *Historie*) can only be an entity to be considered within worldly, social-psychological categories. So liberal theology is ultimately concerned with something understandable in terms of worldly historical categories and cannot therefore be a true theology, since God is absolutely other than the world. The essential stumbling block *(skandalon)* has been lost. [9]

Here, again, we have a point characteristic of, and absolutely essential to, the Bultmannian position. All through his work Bultmann raises, as he is doing here, the question of the relationship between faith (and theology as the explication of faith) and history, where history is understood as that history which historians investigate (*Historie*). Broadly speaking, there are three answers to this question.

First, there is the answer of Christian orthodoxy that, since God was incarnate in a historical person, the revelation of God must be visible to historical investigation when that investigation is properly carried out. This position has been recently revived by Wolfhart Pannenberg who develops his thesis in conscious opposition to that of Bultmann. In his book *Jesus—God and Man,* he argues, for example, that the divinity of Jesus must be visible in the history of Jesus as this is properly investigated by historians, and he argues that this is in fact the case. Jesus made specific claims about himself in that he claimed that salvation depended upon a specific response to himself (Luke 12:8f.: "Everyone who acknowledges me before men, the Son of man also will acknowledge before the angels of God; but he who denies me before men will be denied before the angels of God"). Then God ratified these claims by the resurrection, which was an event within history for which there is adequate historical evidence in the Pauline account of the appearances of the risen Lord (I Cor. 15:3-7). [10]

In light of our discussion in Chapter IV, we can see that Bultmann would make a twofold reply to this position. On the one hand, it depends upon the acceptance of the authenticity of Luke 12:8f., and here we become involved in the ambiguity and relativity of the results of historical research. The authenticity of this saying is hotly debated by New Testament scholars, with the weight of the evidence about equally balanced, and although Bultmann himself tends to accept it, he would never accept the idea of tying a key element in Christian theology to the results of such a debate. Then, on the other hand, the "appearances" are a phenomenon which historians can only investigate as part of the phenomena investigated under the rubrics and categories of the history of religions. They belong under a general category such as "ecstatic visionary experiences," of which they may be particularly interesting or even exceptional examples, but the resurrection as an event guaranteeing the unique status of Jesus cannot be made dependent upon even an exceptional example of a category of events well known from the history of religious. Pannenberg actually tries to meet this point in advance by claiming that primitive Christianity apparently distinguished these appearances from ecstatic visionary experiences, but this only impales him on the other horn of the dilemma because then he is dependent upon the validity of this historical claim and thus subject to the relativities and ambiguities of the results of historical research.

The second answer is that of liberal theology, which is fully prepared to accept the relativity of history. In effect, liberalism recognizes that any historical phenomenon is but one phenomenon among others and does not hesitate to accept the fact, therefore, that the historical Jesus is but one moral man among other moral men. He is unique only in the sense that he represents the best possibility inherent in the very stuff of humanity, an ideal which others may emulate but which no other has in fact achieved. So his spirit challenges other men to emulate his example as his life epitomizes the possibilities for any life.

Bultmann himself represents the third alternative, which is to recognize the ambiguities and relativities of history but to dissociate faith from them. In some way faith has to be associated with an absolute beyond the vicissitudes of history while, at the same time, those aspects of the history of faith which belong intrinsically to the stuff of history are left subject to its ambiguities and relativities. Bultmann achieves this by abandoning the historical Jesus to the vicissitudes of history and by claiming that Christian faith is not in fact necessarily related to that historical Jesus but, rather, is dependent upon something which lies beyond historical investigation, namely, the eschatological act of God in Jesus and in the Christian kerygma. We shall have occasion later to discuss what Bultmann means by the eschatological act of God in the cross and in the kerygma; at the moment our concern is to show that it is for him a means of escaping the dilemma forced upon any Christian theologian who recognizes that the historical Jesus is necessarily as ambiguous and relative as any other historical phenomenon and that this poses real problems for that explication of Christian faith which is theology.

It is hard to see how Bultmann can be faulted at this point. An orthodoxy which insists that the absolute has been revealed in history (when history means that history which historians investigate) finds itself impaled on the horns of an inescapable dilemma. A liberalism which reduces the Jesus who is the concern of faith to one historical phenomenon among others necessarily must accept the fact that Christian faith becomes but one example among many of the religious possibilities open to humanity as humanity. If Christian faith is to justify its claim to uniqueness as the once-for-all revelation of God to man, then it has to have as its central concern something which is within history—otherwise, men could not respond to it—but at the same time beyond history. This is exactly what Bultmann's concepts of eschatology and the kerygma achieve, as we shall see, and it is hard to see any alternative to those of either following Bultmann or abandoning the particularistic claims of Christian faith.

Further points made in Bultmann's 1924 essay which concern us here are in connection with God and with faith. As we should by now expect, in view of what has been said above about God as the wholly other in Bultmann's theology, the essay makes the point that God is not something given, not an object present to human knowledge which like other objects can be known to a greater or less extent. "The concept God necessarily means the abandonment of anything human, the radical negation, questioning and judgment of the human."[11] Since this is the case, then faith can only be a response to the word of God, in which the judgment and grace of God are proclaimed, and it cannot be an act carried out once for all by means of which men achieve justification before God. [12] If it were either of these things it would be human-historical, and hence necessarily relative and ambiguous, and then it could not relate to the absolute, the wholly other, which is God.

Leaving for the next chapter a discussion of Bultmann's understanding of faith, we use this opportunity to say something of his concept of God. It is evident from what has been said already that Bultmann is keenly aware of what has been called the "infinite qualitative difference" between God and the world, a concept that ultimately goes back to Kierkegaard.[13] For him as for Barth and dialectical theology in general, God is "wholly other" than the world: he cannot be an object of human knowledge; he cannot be a "given" to humanity. These themes are sounded in the 1924 essay we have been considering and they are sounded throughout his work. We shall refer briefly to two further essays which relate to this subject, "What Sense Is There to Speak of God?"[14] and "The Idea of God and Modern Man."[15] They are separated by almost forty years, being dated 1925 and 1963 respectively, but they exhibit a consistency of concept which is characteristic of Bultmann.

In the first of these essays Bultmann argues that we can no more talk *about* God than we can talk *about* love. As with love, we either know God or we do not; he is not a subject for human discussion. He is the wholly other over and beyond the human, but at the same time he is the reality which determines our existence. This is a paradox, and an essential paradox. At one and the same time God is the wholly other, who cannot be the subject of human knowledge, and the reality who determines human existence. "That God, who determines my existence, at the same time is the wholly other, can only mean that he confronts me, the sinner, as *the* wholly other; that, insofar as I am world, he confronts me as *the* wholly other."[16] The point is that man in the world is a sinner and as such cannot possibly know God, yet, at the same time, God seeks man out, so to speak. Man as a sinner cannot know God, God as the wholly other cannot be the subject of human knowledge, but man *as man* can know that his whole existence is determined by God and man *as a Christian* can find himself confronted by God in the Christian proclamation *(kerygma)*.

The essay we have been quoting was written in 1925, when Bultmann had known Heidegger for some three years, and it already shows the way in which his thinking was being influenced by that philosopher's existentialism. Bultmann has learned to think of human existence as inauthentic in the world apart from God and as authentic in the world only insofar as it is determined by God. At the same time man cannot find God, the wholly other; he can only be confronted by him. He is confronted by him in the Christian proclamation (and only in the Christian proclamation, this being a stumbling block [*skandalon*] to the world) and as he responds to this proclamation (this response is "faith"), he finds that authentic existence which is life in faith. Here we have two things being said. In the first place we have the claim that human existence is such that true human existence, authentic existence, is a possibility in principle (Bultmann's technical term is "ontological possibility") for all humanity, but it is a possibility in fact ("ontic possibility") only to a man who responds to the Christian proclamation and finds his existence determined by God. We shall return to this theme later; for the moment we are more concerned with the second thing, namely, the paradox of God as the wholly other who cannot be the subject of human knowledge and yet who confronts every man in the Christian proclamation and who ultimately determines all human existence. This is a paradox which is essential to Bultmann's theology and it is difficult to see how one can resolve it without giving up something that is essential to theology as the explication of Christian faith. If God is not the wholly other, then he is not God, but as a subject of human knowledge one object among many objects. At the same time, if God does not determine human existence, then there is no point to faith in him, and there must therefore be some way of relating the wholly other to the human. Bultmann does this with his concept of

51

God encountering man in the kerygma, the Christian proclamation, and it is difficult to think of a better way of doing it and quite impossible to think of one more in keeping with the New Testament. Here, as everywhere else in his theology, Bultmann is consciously being influenced by the New Testament; for example, Romans 10:14-17:

> But how are men to call upon him in whom they have not believed? And how are they to believe in him of whom they have never heard? And how are they to hear without a preacher? And how can men preach unless they are sent? As it is written, "How beautiful are the feet of those who preach good news!" But they have not all heeded the gospel; for Isaiah says, "Lord, who has believed what he has heard from us?" So faith comes from what is heard, and what is heard comes by the preaching of Christ.

In his 1963 essay, we find Bultmann quite unperturbed by the radical theology of J. A. T. Robinson's *Honest to God* and Gabriel Vahanian's *The Death of God* and still maintaining the essential thing for him: "Only the idea of God which can find, which can seek and find, the *unconditional in the conditional,* the beyond in the here, the transcendent in the present at hand, as possibility of encounter, is possible for modern man. It then remains to keep oneself open at any time for the *encounter with God in the world, in time.*"[17] Saved by this paradox of the wholly other present for encounter in the Christian proclamation, Bultmann has no problem with the radical theology of the "death of God" and he could, and does, quite cheerfully contemplate with Herbert Braun the possibility of not talking about God at all, but about "the whence of my being agitated," for this is the essential thing: God is the determinant of my existence, the whence of my being agitated.

We now return to one last point from Bultmann's 1924 essay, "Liberal Theology and the Newest Theological Movement." It follows from what we have already seen that for Bultmann the historical Jesus can never be the origin or central concern of Christian faith as he was for Harnack and for liberal theology. As a historical figure he is as relative a phenomenon as all other historical phenomena, and historical knowledge of him is as ambiguous as any other historical knowledge. Such relativity and ambiguity can never be the source of faith in God, the wholly other. "One who seeks love and forgiveness is not helped by the recognition that others claim to have known love and forgiveness. That claim could be an illusion. It may be that Jesus' love for sinners could help to shatter the mistrust one tends to feel for someone better than oneself, but even then my sins are not forgiven for I stand in my sins directly before God."[18] This is the case for Bultmann with all historical knowledge, including such knowledge of Jesus; it can affect the knower as a human being in some ways, but it cannot mediate knowledge of God, and it cannot therefore be the source or central concern of faith.

Despite this limitation on the significance of knowledge of the historical Jesus, Bultmann did write a book on Jesus, published in 1926 and translated into English as *Jesus and the Word.* One might ask why he should write such a book and the answer would be twofold. On the one hand, he had in his *History of the Synoptic Tradition* formulated a methodology for working back through the teaching material presented in the Synoptic Gospels (Matthew, Mark and Luke) to the earliest form of that material known to the church and then for determining what part of that material may, with some confidence, be ascribed to Jesus. In this respect his work was epoch-making;[19] now, for the first time, a truly historical presentation of the teaching of Jesus was possible and it was natural that Bultmann should make such a presentation. (His book is concerned with the teaching of Jesus rather than with his life as such.) Then, on the other hand, he had come to accept an existentialist view of history in terms of which historical knowledge has a very definite significance, namely, that of challenging the knower at the level of self-understanding, or understanding of existence. This is a very real significance:

... when I speak of the teaching or thought of Jesus . . . the ideas are understood in the light of the concrete situation of a man living in time; as his interpretation of his own existence in the midst of change, uncertainty, decision; as an expression of the possibility of comprehending this life; as the effort to gain clear insight into the contingencies and necessities of his own existence. When we encounter the words of Jesus in history, *we* do not judge *them* by a philosophical system with reference to their rational validity; *they* meet *us* with the question of how we are to interpret our own existence.[20]

In this respect the words of Jesus are not different from the words of other significant figures from the past. All words which reflect the understanding of existence of a significant individual from the past challenge us at the level of our understanding of our own existence, those of Jesus no less, and no more, than those of Plato, Shakespeare or Goethe.

If we use here the terms which we discussed in Chapter IV then Bultmann is saying that the teaching of Jesus can become historic (history as *Geschichte*) in that it reflects an understanding of existence which can challenge us at the level of our understanding of our own existence, at the level of our historicity. When he speaks of encountering the words of Jesus in history he is talking of words become historic and of our encountering them in terms of our historicity. The history to which he is referring is the *Geschichte-Geschichtlichkeit* continuum.

It is most important to stress here the two points that, in the first place, Jesus is in this respect no different from Plato, Goethe or Shakespeare, and that, in the second place, the challenge of the encounter with the words of Jesus to our self-understanding is *not* a challenge that can lead to the self-understanding of faith.

Bultmann consistently regards the earthly Jesus as a truly historical figure and as such as relative as any other such figure. He was a Jewish apocalyptic preacher challenging his contemporaries to radical obedience in view of the imminence of the coming of the Reign of God. In his book, *Primitive Christianity,* Bultmann includes Jesus in the section dealing with Judaism and not in that concerned with Christianity. As Plato is an outstanding Greek philosopher and Goethe and Shakespeare outstanding poets and playwrights, so Jesus is an outstanding Jewish apocalyptic preacher. And just as the words of Plato, Goethe or Shakespeare can challenge us at the level of our self-understanding so also can those of Jesus. The words of Goethe and Shakespeare, of Plato and Jesus, can all be encountered in that realm where the historic confronts us at the level of our historicity. But this challenge can never be that which offers us the possibility of authentic existence. In Chapter III we saw that Bultmann affirms that authentic existence is only possible on the basis of a response to the challenge of "the word of God which proclaims His action in Jesus Christ," and in the next chapter we shall go into this in more detail and find that by "the word of God which proclaims His action in Jesus Christ," Bultmann means the kerygma (proclamation) of the church. The words of Jesus are not such a proclamation and so cannot offer the possibility of authentic existence any more than can the words of Plato, Goethe or Shakespeare. Similarly, a presentation of the words of Jesus in *Jesus and the Word* is not kerygma and cannot therefore be the challenge to that response which is faith.

So the historical Jesus is of very limited significance to the theology of Rudolf Bultmann. Like other historical figures, he can challenge one's understanding of existence, and in point of historical fact, he is one presupposition among others for the theology of the New Testament and hence for Christian theology altogether. But he is not of constitutive significance for that theology, for Christian faith is response not to the message of Jesus but to the message of the church about him.

The contrast between the message of Jesus and the message about Jesus is one to which Bultmann returns again and again. His favorite way of expressing it is to say that the Proclaimer became the Proclaimed. Jesus proclaimed the imminent coming of the Reign of God, and by Reign of God he meant that eschatological act of God by which the old world comes to an end and the new world is established. The church, on the other hand, did not proclaim the Reign of God as eschatological event; but she proclaimed Jesus Christ as eschatological event. The claim of the church's kerygma is that in Jesus, God has acted to bring the old to an end and to make the new possible. Here a double shift has taken place. First, the Proclaimer of the Reign of God as eschatological event has become the one Proclaimed as eschatological event, and, second, the eschatological event is no longer imminent but already past: God *has* acted to bring the old to an end. He has acted in the event of Jesus Christ, more specifically in his cross, and he continues to act to make the power of this act available to men at the level of their history through the kerygma (proclamation) of the church.

# VI

# The Kerygma, Faith and Self-Understanding

Kerygma, faith and self-understanding belong together in Bultmann's theology, and although we ended Chapter V on the note of the kerygma, it will be more convenient now to begin with "faith" and then move on to "kerygma."

We take as a starting point a passage from the Epilogue to volume two of Bultmann's *Theology of the New Testament,* where we find him saying: "But the most important thing is that basic insight that the theological thoughts of the New Testament are the unfolding of faith itself growing out of that new understanding of God, the world, and man which is conferred in and by faith—or, as it can also be phrased: *out of one's new self-understanding.*"[1] In light of the discussion in the preceding chapters, we are in a position to appreciate the meaning of this sentence. We have seen that, for Bultmann, theology—and hence "the theological thoughts of the New Testament"—is the careful self-interpretation of faith or, as he puts it here, "the unfolding of faith itself." Again, we can appreciate what he means by those two equivalent expressions, "that new understanding of God, the world, and man," and "one's new self-understanding": the reference is to "authentic existence." The particular note to which we wish to call attention now, however, is the relationship between this "new self-understanding" and faith: it is conferred in and by faith—and for Bultmann *only* in and by faith—and in turn faith grows out of it. Faith, then, is both that initial response to an existential encounter by means of which the new self-understanding is first attained, and it is also the continuing responses to further encounters, responses which are at one and the same time made possible by that self-understanding and further nurture it.

The matter becomes clearer if we read further in the Epilogue, for we find the following careful statement:

> In the New Testament faith is not understood as a self-understanding arising spontaneously out of human existence but as an understanding made possible by God, opened up by his dealings with men. Faith is not choosing to understand one's self in one of several possible ways that are universally available to man but is man's response to God's word which encounters him in the proclamation of Jesus Christ. It is *faith in the kerygma,* which tells of God's dealing in the man Jesus of Nazareth.[2]

This is a statement of what Bultmann finds in the New Testament but it is also, and at the same time, a statement of major aspects of Bultmann's theological position. Statements of similar import to this one could be found throughout his work, for example, in the 1929 essay, "The Concept of Revelation in the New Testament," and in the 1930 essay, "Historicity of Man and Faith" (both now to be found in *Existence and Faith*) or in *Jesus Christ and Mythology* (1958). But we shall stay with the present statement, originally written in 1950, for it is a good one and a consideration of it will take us to the heart of the matter.

In the first place, this statement shows us something of the range of meaning which Bultmann gives to the word "faith." When he says, ". . . faith is . . . an understanding made possible by God," he clearly uses the word to denote the self-understanding of faith, that authentic existence which faith alone makes possible. But when he says, "Faith . . . is man's response to God's word . . . ," he equally clearly uses it for that response to the encounter with God which makes possible that self-understanding, that authentic existence. This is not simply terminological inexactitude, a clumsy use of words but, rather, an indication of how deeply Bultmann concentrates upon faith itself. For him faith is both the initial response and also the existence which thereby becomes possible for man in the world, because that existence must itself be an expression of the response and constantly demands further responses.

Bultmann never tires of making these points. In discussing faith as faith in God as creator, for example, he says: "Faith in the creator can never be possessed once for all as a reassuring insight, but must constantly be won and realized anew."[3] In *Jesus Christ and Mythology* he claims: "In faith man understands himself anew," and then goes on: "In faith man understands himself *ever* anew. This new self-understanding can be maintained only as a continual response to the word . . . "[4] In other words, the initial response must constantly be renewed by further responses. At the same time the response is expressed in the self-understanding to which it gives rise, and that self-understanding in turn is an expression of the response of faith, which is why it is the "self-understanding of faith." Lutheran theologians are brought up on a way of speaking about faith as both the act of believing and that which is believed. So here Bultmann, for whom faith is that response which makes possible true self-understanding, quite naturally speaks of faith as both the initial response and that self-understanding. At the same time there is more to it than that, for Bultmann also constantly stresses the fact that the self-understanding must be an appropriate expression of that which is appropriated in the moment of response. In his essay, "The Historicity of Man and Faith," for example, he accepts a contention of Gogarten that the response by which authenticity is achieved is a response to love (of God) and must constantly be expressed in love (for the neighbor), and for the remainder of the essay speaks of "the man of faith and love."[5] In the same year (1930) he returned to this theme in an essay. *"Das christliche Gebot der Nächstenliebe"* ("The Christian Commandment 'Love Thy Neighbor' ") in which he made the points that love is not so much a series of acts as a way of being, and that it is a way of being made possible only by the forgiving love of God encountered in that word of God to which faith is the response.[6] We can see, therefore, that when "faith" is used of both the response and the self-understanding, then a great deal is being said.

In the paragraph from the Epilogue to the *Theology of the New Testament* we are presently considering, faith is "man's response to God's word which encounters him," and here we arrive at Bultmann's understanding of the kerygma. We can see that in this paragraph "God's word . . . in the proclamation of Jesus Christ [by the church]" is the same as "the kerygma which tells of God's dealings in the man Jesus of Nazareth." But we must take this opportunity to mention a point that we shall attempt to make clear in our subsequent discussion, namely, that "Jesus Christ" in the first statement is not a synonym for "the man Jesus of Nazareth" in the second. The first is the risen Lord present in the kerygma as eschatological event; the second is the historical Jesus whose cross is at one and the same time historical happening and eschatological event.

We now reapproach the matter of the relationship between Bultmann and Heidegger, and we must begin by stressing a point that we only mentioned in passing before, namely, the distinction between a possibility in principle and a possibility in fact, to use the technical terms: between an ontological possibility and an ontic possibility. For Heidegger authentic existence is a possibility in principle, he can describe it and indicate its place in his analysis of human existence, and it is also a possibility in fact: by resolute decision in face of the inevitability of death a man can achieve it.[7] Bultmann, as we saw, calls this "a resolution of despair" and denies that it can lead to authentic existence. For Bultmann authentic existence is a possibility in principle but it is not a possibility in fact, unless God makes it such. In the words he uses in the paragraph from the Epilogue, the self-understanding of faith (authentic existence) does not arise "spontaneously out of human existence" but is "made possible by God, opened up by His dealings with man." Man is in fact fallen, he has denied his necessary dependence upon the creator, and the "resolution of despair" cannot be the answer to the dilemma in which he now finds himself. The possibility of decision which marks the transition to authentic existence is therefore only ontological, not ontic—a possibility in principle, but not in fact. A philosopher can describe the possibility but not make it available to man.

The fundamental distinction between Bultmann and Heidegger is not to be found in the view of man, nor in the view of the distinction between inauthentic and authentic existence. The distinction is to be found in the view of the possibility for authentic existence: for Heidegger it arises "spontaneously out of human existence," for Bultmann it is "made possible by God."

The importance of this point is much greater than that it is a distinction between Heidegger and Bultmann, for here we have one of the points at which the debate about Bultmann's theological position becomes a debate about the possibility of developing a Christian theology at all. Theology is an academic, scientific discipline; as such, it necessarily attempts to maintain an academic and scientific integrity. This means that it must necessarily wrestle with the findings of philosophy—and of the natural and social sciences—as it carries on its particular task. True, these "findings" change from age to age and from generation to generation but then so does theology. It is possible, of course, simply to repeat parrot-fashion the theology of a figure from the past, some great Reformation or Puritan divine for example, or simply to ignore philosophy or science altogether as ultimately irrelevant. But either of these alternatives means abandoning the possibility of true communication with the present, and Bultmann would most emphatically repudiate them, as would the tradition of German Protestant theology in which he stands. However, if one is to take the philosophy and science of the age seriously in one's theologizing, then how far can one maintain the particularity of Christian faith? This is a most important question and one which Bultmann boldly confronts. Part of his answer is the point which concerns us here, namely, to accept the philosophical analysis of human existence as indicating the "possibility in principle" of authentic existence but to go on from there to claim that only God can make authentic existence a "possibility in fact." How far it is possible to claim this is a good question. If it is not possible then an even better question is that of whether or not Christian faith can be maintained at all as anything more than one among many possibilities for achieving authenticity in human existence. This latter is the question which Bultmann has seen and to which he is attempting to develop an answer. These matters will concern us again later; for the moment we return to our descriptive discussion of Bultmann's theology.

For Bultmann authentic existence, true self-understanding, is made possible only by God, and it is made possible by him through his word: "Faith . . . is man's response to God's word which encounters him in the proclamation of Jesus Christ. It is *faith in the kerygma* which tells of God's dealings in the man Jesus of Nazareth." "God's word," "the proclamation of Jesus Christ," "the kerygma"—these are references to what is for Bultmann the most important thing of all. They are references to what is for him the means by which God makes himself known to men and the means by which he makes authentic existence possible for them. We must now come to grips, therefore, with what Bultmann means by the kerygma, the proclamation of Jesus Christ, the word of God.

In order to explore Bultmann's understanding of "kerygma" we leave the Epilogue to the *Theology of the New Testament* and turn to the essay, "General Truths and Christian Proclamation," which we shall supplement by references to two further essays, "New Testament and Mythology," and "The Primitive Christian Kerygma and the Historical Jesus."

In the summary of his understanding of Christian kerygma or proclamation in the first section of the essay "General Truths and Christian Proclamation,"[8] Bultmann begins by making the point that this proclamation is spoken by a man, the preacher, and yet at the same time it is, paradoxically, the authoritative word of God. As the proclaimer of this word, the preacher stands over against the congregation as God's representative. At the same time the preacher stands before God as one of the congregation and proclaims the word to himself.

That which makes the sermon proclamation or kerygma is that it communicates an event, "namely the event of the revelation of God's grace that has occurred in Jesus Christ." This is a point which Bultmann constantly stresses. In the paragraph from the Epilogue quoted above he wrote of the kerygma "which tells of God's dealing in Jesus of Nazareth." In *New Testament and Mythology,* it is "the event of Jesus Christ" which is "the revelation of the love of God," which "makes man free from himself and free to be himself . . . ." [9] What is it then, this "event of Jesus Christ," the proclamation of which makes the sermon kerygma?

In answering this question Bultmann focuses his attention sharply upon the event of the cross. For him the death of Jesus on the cross is the one all-important historical event, the one actual happening within the realm of secular or world history with which Christian faith cannot dispense. It is not the fact of death by crucifixion in itself that matters—God could have made the death the eschatological event whatever its mode—but the historical fact of the death itself. Bultmann would say that so far as the kerygma is concerned it does not matter how Jesus lived, but only *that* he lived; it does not matter *how* Jesus died, but only *that* he died. It is not the "what" or the "how" of Jesus' life and death that matters, but only "that" he lived and died. The German word for "that" is *dass* and this is therefore Bultmann's famous contention that only the *dass* of Jesus and his cross are significant to the kerygma and hence to Christian faith. The kerygma necessarily presupposes the historicity of Jesus and his cross, but it is proclaiming Jesus as the Christ, it is proclaiming that cross as both a historical and the eschatological event, and the "what" and the "how" of the historical Jesus and his cross are not of concern to the kerygma. [10]

Bultmann, then, focuses his attention sharply upon the historicity of Jesus and his cross as the necessary starting point for an understanding of the "event of Jesus Christ," the proclamation of which makes a sermon kerygma. Then he goes on to argue that as it is taken up into the kerygma, "the historical event of the cross acquires cosmic dimensions."[11] By this he means that the cross is now understood and proclaimed as "the judgment of this world and the defeat of the rulers of this world" (I Cor. 2:6ff.); it is now "the judgment and deliverance of man"; it now has for man "its redemptive aspect." [12]

Another way of saying this, and a way more characteristic of Bultmann, is to say that "the cross is not just an event of the past which can be contemplated, but is the eschatological event in and beyond time,"[13] or, "the kerygma proclaims [the historical] Jesus as the Christ, as the eschatological event."[14] As we have pointed out in Chapter IV, the eschatological event is for Bultmann, as for early Christian apocalyptic, that event in which God finally acts to bring about the End, to judge and redeem mankind. But for Bultmann this eschatological event is not the coming of Jesus on a cloud to judge the quick and the dead; it is the proclamation in which man encounters his one and only opportunity for authentic existence.

The cross of Jesus is therefore both a historical event—Jesus was crucified under Pontius Pilate—and an eschatological event. It is the eschatological event because, as it is proclaimed in the kerygma, it confronts man with his only possibility for authentic existence. The cross is "the eschatological event in and beyond time." It is "in time" because as it is proclaimed in the kerygma it confronts man in the concrete historicity of his being-in-the-world. It is "beyond time" because it is the means by which God, the wholly other who limits and determines human existence and who himself is beyond history and time, has chosen to offer man a possibility not ontically (in fact) present to him in history and time itself.

The eschatological event of Jesus Christ is therefore that moment on the cross where history and eschatology intersect, where time and eternity coincide for one fate-laden moment. This is the event in which God has chosen finally to reveal himself as the one who determines human existence and as the one who offers man his only possibility for true self-understanding in his being-in-the-world.

But there is more to it than this, for an event in the past, however fate-laden, cannot confront a man in his concrete being-in-the-world unless it can become for him an event within his own personal, concrete history. This is what, for Bultmann, the proclamation itself achieves. The proclamation of the eschatological event does more than call attention to an event in the past and offer an interpretation of it in terms of its significance for man. The proclamation of the cross repeats the event of the cross in that it makes it a reality in the present of the hearer. In the kerygma the event of the cross is not only an occurrence in past history; it also becomes an occurrence in the present, concrete, personal history of the hearer in that it confronts him as address, as the actual challenge to decision which will make possible the new self-understanding. So the cross is not only the eschatological event in that it is the event by means of which God chose to visit and redeem mankind, to make authentic existence a possibility in fact; it is also the eschatological event because in the proclamation it reoccurs in the concrete historical present of the believer. As he summarizes the matter in "General Truths and Christian Proclamation":

> True, there is something "communicated" in a genuine sermon, namely an event, the event of the revelation of God's grace that has occurred in Jesus Christ. The remarkable thing, however, is that one must really say not the revelation which *has occurred,* but the revelation which *is occurring.* For this communication does not make known a past historical fact; rather, the paradox is that, in this

"communication," the occurrence of revelation takes place anew, in that a historical event is proclaimed as the eschatological event.[15]

So far as Bultmann is concerned there is the ultimate and all-important paradox that an event, the cross of Christ, can be at one and the same time both historical and eschatological, and that it can become eschatological only by being both an event in the past history of the world and the present history of the man in the world to whom the kerygma becomes personal address.

The kerygma proclaimed by the church and the response of faith by the man to whom this becomes personal address make possible the authentic existence which is the self-understanding of faith. Bultmann tends to stay close to an exegesis of the New Testament, especially to Paul and John. We shall take as our example the essay, "Man between the Times according to the New Testament," originally published in 1952.[16]

In this essay Bultmann is concerned, first, to inquire into the significance of the acceptance of the challenge of the message of Jesus by those who heard it. That message is one of "the certainty of the unconditionedness of the divine demand and the divine grace" and it expresses "the certainty that he, Jesus, has to proclaim these realities as something new, unheard of, and definitive."[17] Jesus proclaimed the imminence, indeed the in-breaking, of the Reign of God as eschatological event (divine grace) and challenged his hearers to respond to this by radical obedience to the divine demand. He used "the mythological notion of the end of the old, and the beginning of the new aeon" but the import of his message was such that for the hearer "who lets God be his God, the past is extinguished and the future is open."[18] In other words, the hearer of the message of Jesus who responded correctly to its challenge achieved authentic existence.

There are two points to which attention must be called here. The first concerns Bultmann's understanding of authentic existence: it is freedom from the past and openness for the future. Man is fallen, imprisoned by the past, unable to respond to the challenge of the future because in the future he will always go on experiencing only the futility of his past and present. The reason for this is that he has rejected God and made gods of the world and the things of the world. But if he will let God be his God then all this will change and the future will be open to him, because now he will be enabled to make the decision which will lead to authentic existence. The second point is that Bultmann is here conceding that Jesus made authentic existence possible for the hearers of his message. We mention this only in passing at this time but we shall return to it later, for it is a point on which Bultmann has been challenged. The questions have been raised: If Jesus made authentic existence possible for his hearers why cannot encounter with the words of Jesus at the level of the historic (*Geschichte—Geschichtlichkeit*) mediate authentic existence to us? Further, if this is possible, then is not the historical Jesus more significant for faith than Bultmann will concede? We shall discuss these questions later; for the moment we stay with Bultmann's understanding of authentic existence.

In the essay, "Man between the Times," Bultmann moves from Jesus to the early church: mostly, although not exclusively, to Paul, John and Ignatius. Here he develops the theme that the man of faith is the one for whom "through Christ the old aeon of sin has been brought to an end and the new aeon of salvation established."[19] This is mythological language but its import is clear: the old aeon of sin is "my particular past in which I was a sinner," the new aeon of salvation is "the future for which I am freed. . .my future."[20]

The crux of the matter for Bultmann is that man, natural man, is a sinner. "Sin is to want to live out of one's self, out of one's own power, rather than out of radical surrender to God, to what he demands, gives, and sends,"[21] and this is that which afflicts all men and makes authentic existence impossible for any man. For this sin only God can free man and "it is from this sin that the grace of God frees the man who opens himself to it in radical self-surrender, i.e. in faith."[22] Through the eschatological event of the cross as proclaimed in the kerygma, God does free a man from sin and make authentic existence possible for him. But this authentic existence is still an existence in the world and this is expressed in the New Testament and the early church by the concept of "interim." In the message of Jesus the hearer is challenged, in that authentic existence is made possible for him. However, he lives out this possibility only for a brief period which will be brought to an end by the coming of the Son of man.[23] The men of the New Testament proclaim the kerygma which sets men free, but they also regard this freedom as one that is to be exercised in an interim which will be brought to an end by the coming of Christ as Son of man. Bultmann refuses to take these statements literally. Neither the proclamation by Jesus of the coming of the Son of man nor that by the church of the coming of Jesus as Son of man is a literal description of a reality to be expected in history. What these proclamations point to is the reality of life within history. The "interim" is not chronological but qualitative: even authentic existence is existence in the world and as such will always have an element of tension about it. At this point Bultmann turns to Paul and especially to I Corinthians 7:29-31, a passage he never tires of quoting:

> I mean, brethren, the appointed time has grown very short; from now on, let those who have wives live as though they had none, and those who mourn as though they were not mourning, and those who rejoice as though they were not rejoicing, and those who buy as though they had no goods, and those who deal with the world as though they had no dealings with it. For the form of this world is passing away.

A key to Bultmann's understanding of authentic existence or the self-understanding of faith is that it can be summed up as a combination of the indicative and imperative: "You can" and "You must." By the eschatological event of the cross as proclaimed in the kerygma a man is set free from his past, I am set free from my past: "I can." At the same time radical obedience is demanded of that man, of me: "I must." Even

68

so it will be "as if not" but nonetheless *it will be*. Apart from the kerygma there can be only meaninglessness and despair; in response to the kerygma there is the paradoxical glory of authentic existence in the world in which a man finds himself at one and the same time justified and yet a sinner.

There are, thus, four notes which Bultmann constantly sounds in his discussions of the self-understanding of faith. The first is from the New Testament, the "as though not" passage, I Corinthians 7:29-31, which we quoted above. In his very perceptive introduction to Bultmann's theology in *Existence and Faith,* Schubert Ogden calls attention to the frequency with which it is quoted in Bultmann's writings and then goes on to say, quite correctly: "What is clearly presupposed by the notion that the Christian's participation in the world is subject to the reservation 'as though not' is the dialectical relation of God and world which is the inmost meaning of Bultmann's theology."[24] Just as God at one and the same time radically transcends the world as the wholly other and yet confronts man in the world through the kerygma, so also the man who attains the self-understanding of faith lives in the world of radical historicity "as though not," and it is precisely "in this attitude of 'as though not' that Christian freedom from the world consists."[25] The second note comes from the Reformation and it is a phrase which Bultmann quotes as often as he does the "as though not" passage, namely, the Lutheran *simul iustus, et peccator* ("at one and the same time justified and a sinner").[26] The third is from existentialist philosophy, the concept of a fundamental decision which marks the transition to authentic existence, but which has to be renewed in the thousand decisions that being-in-the-world of "care" will demand. The fourth is the paradoxical relationship of the indicative and the imperative, the enabling "You can" and the demanding "You must." All these are for Bultmann different ways of saying the same thing; they all express "the paradox that Christian existence is at the same time an eschatological unworldly being and a historical being." [27]

# VII

# Demythologizing and the Existential Interpretation of the Documents of Faith

*Entmythologizierung*—"demythologizing": in German or in English it is an ugly mouthful, but it is the word above all others which is associated with Bultmann's theological program. In 1941 he published a programmatic essay—an essay announcing a proposed program—"The New Testament and Mythology" and from that moment forward his name became a household word in the world of theology and the church. Today there is a whole literature upon the subject, a literature so vast that no one can keep track of it. Fortunately the basic issues and ideas involved are not too difficult to grasp in view of Bultmann's fundamental theological thrust but they do have to be carefully sorted out, especially in view of the misunderstanding that has only too often beclouded the discussion.

The basic impulse behind Bultmann's proposal is quite simply the desire of a preacher to communicate with his congregation. He wants to be able to present the challenge of the Christian gospel effectively to the men of his day, for he is concerned that they should make the decision between faith and unfaith and so attain that faith which is "man's response to the proclamation of the word of God's grace, a word whose origin and credentials are to be found in the New Testament."[1] In order to do this, Bultmann claims that we have to go to work at two different levels and in two different ways. On the one hand, we must study the proclamation itself so that we may most effectively present it today and, on the other hand, we must study the man with whom we wish to communicate so as to be able to help be ready to hear the word of God addressed to him. The process by means of which these things are achieved is that of "demythologizing."

We have to start with that which is essential for Bultmann, namely, that "God encounters us in His word—i.e. in a particular word, in the proclamation inaugurated with Jesus Christ."[2] He formulated that sentence carefully in response to his critics and it does, for him, express the heart of the matter. God is known as he addresses us in his word and in no other way. "True, God encounters us at all times and in all places, but he cannot be seen everywhere unless his Word comes as well and makes the moment of revelation intelligible to us in its own light."[3] This word addresses us in encounter ever and ever again but always on a specific occasion, "whether it be in the church's proclamation, or in the Bible mediated through the Church as the Word of God addressed to me, or through the word of my fellow Christian."[4]

This is Bultmann's understanding of the proclamation, the kerygma, which we discussed in Chapter VI. The points he wants to stress here are that this is the *only* way in which God encounters us and that the encounter is *always* a concrete one at the level of our historicity. Of course he is prepared to use "word" widely (it can be a word heard or read thirty years ago and suddenly remembered), but he is not prepared to concede any other form of encounter with God—"unless the Word comes as well"—and he will always insist that the encounter be historical, that is, concrete at the level of the historicity of our existence.

The word of God is, then, "an event encountered in history" and "this event is Jesus Christ."[5] The word is that proclamation which has its starting point in the historical event of the cross of Jesus, in which Jesus Christ is present as eschatological event, and by means of which he encounters us at the level of our historicity. This is the essential thing and it matters not whether we read it in the New Testament, hear it in church, or are caught up short by it in the testimony of a Martin Luther King, Jr. Always it will have the same constants: the proclaimer Jesus whose cross is at one and the same time history and eschatology and the proclaimed Jesus Christ who encounters us in our history.

This is the absolute crux of the matter so far as Bultmann is concerned. The paradox of the cross as at one and the same time historical and eschatological event; the presence of Jesus Christ in the kerygma as eschatological event; the reality of the encounter with the Jesus Christ proclaimed as eschatological event and in terms of the concrete actuality of our own historicity. He returns to these themes over and over again and is forever concerned that his hearers and followers, his opponents and critics, should grasp that this is what he wants above all to say. The whole purpose of his proposed demythologizing is to clear away obstacles which prevent men from hearing these things.

The fact is that the essential Christian message has been expressed by the use of concepts which once had meaning and reality but which now no longer do so. For example, Jesus proclaimed the coming of the Son of man as the means by which God would act to end the old and begin the new, and the church proclaimed the coming of Jesus as that Son of man. But the idea of this coming depends upon the three-story view of the universe—the earth with the heavens above and hell below—and upon such things as a cloud acting as a kind of celestial elevator. Although this kind of thing is to be found in the New Testament (e.g., in Acts I), if taken literally it is nonsense, but it is actually myth and it is to be taken as myth. For Bultmann, myth is a way of talking about God in human terms, or, as he likes to put it, "of the other side in terms of this side." So in this example of the three-story universe we have ultimately a way of talking about the transcendence of God, but the terms are human: the concept of spatial distance, of "above" and "below." Similarly it is concerned with God as the one who ultimately determines human existence, but this again is now expressed in terms of that which the humans of the day could conceive, of a "Man" coming on a cloud with supernatural beings (angels) to help him, etc. This particular way of talking about God and his control over the destiny of man is not one which the modern man can possibly accept. He knows that the world is not the center of a three-story universe and for him the idea of supernatural beings descending from the sky belongs in the realm of science fiction!

The heart of Bultmann's demythologizing program lies here: in the recognition that the Bible and the church talk about God in terms of myth and that these mythical terms are unacceptable to modern man and hence hinder him from hearing what is truly being said. There are two things that need to be emphasized, namely, Bultmann's understanding of myth and his contention that the world of nature and of history is a closed world in which God cannot be directly known.

Bultmann's understanding of myth is not one that takes into account recent studies of the role of myth and symbol in religious or literary language and it is indeed open to criticism by the historian of religion or the literary critic. But then Bultmann is not attempting to make a contribution to the study of myth and symbol; he is attempting to make the proclamation of the New Testament and of the church intelligible to modern man. For him anything that speaks of the "other side in terms of this side" is myth. So he would include in this category, for example, such things as "the biblical doctrine that death is the punishment for sin," "the doctrine of the atonement . . . [that] the guilt of one man can be expiated by the death of another," "the resurrection of Jesus," "the pre-existence of Christ, with its corollary of man's translation into a celestial realm of light."[6]

All these are mythical statements and our problem is to interpret their meaning to a man who must take them seriously—so the Christian preacher would claim—but who cannot take them literally. Now it is possible to argue that such a definition of myth is too broad and clumsy but it cannot be gainsaid that all these are statements to be found in the New Testament and that what Bultmann is looking for is a way of handling *all such statements in the New Testament.* He is not concerned to clarify the nature and function of myth and symbol in religious thought but to interpret the New Testament, and he has a right to be heard and to be judged by his effectiveness at his chosen task. However, I would be doing less than justice to my readers—or to the integrity which Bultmann would be the first to demand of me—if I did not say that this is one of the few points at which I believe Bultmann to be vulnerable to criticism. This understanding of myth is perhaps too broad and does perhaps do less than justice to the function of myth in religious discourse. But if that is the case, then it means that we have to go further in the direction toward which Bultmann has pointed us—and he would be the first to cheer us on our way!

The second point we need to emphasize is one on which Bultmann is not at all vulnerable; on the contrary, here lies his great strength: the world of nature and of history *is* a closed world in which God cannot be directly known. Bultmann's greatest contribution to the future of theology probably lies in the fact that he has developed a theological position which takes this fact seriously. The natural world is one in which the findings of the natural sciences have to be taken as all-important, and it is many a long year now since the natural scientist has had any need of God as a working hypothesis. Nothing is more pathetic than generations of theologians finding God in a realm which the natural scientists of their day have not managed to explore, only to find that the next generation does explore it. It is not that there are not unexplored areas of ultimate origins or uncertainty where the idea of God actively working in the natural world could not take temporary refuge; to his credit Bultmann has here never based his views on the conviction that science knows everything, or tomorrow will know everything. It is that the very idea of God as an effective cause at the level of the natural

74

world is simply and basically incompatible with a true concept of God. Each person must provide his own illustrations of this point—I was involved in the Second World War and there is for me something theologically obscene about the idea that God was responsible for the good weather that facilitated the evacuation from Dunkirk or the bad weather that hindered the Allies' invasion of Europe. One of the great things about the Bultmannian theology is that it takes a firm stand against this kind of nonsense! Nor does the matter change if we switch to the world of history. All past history is ambiguous, including that of Jesus, and all future history will be equally so. There never has been an event at the level of the history of the world that was unambiguous and there never will be one. But again here Bultmann does not rest his case on the inability of historians to discover an unambiguous historical event; he rests it on the fundamental—and completely correct!—insight that if God were known in terms of an unambiguous historical event, he would simply become one historical cause among others, and then cease to be God.

It is at this point that Bultmann presents his greatest challenge to the theologians. He challenges us to recognize once and for all that the world of nature is the realm of the natural scientist and that the world of history is the realm of the scientific historian, and that neither the scientist nor the historian is ever going to be able to say one word about God. There is an infinite qualitative difference between God and the world of nature and history, and theology must start from that point. The world of nature and history is the world of history as *Historie*: there is also the world of history as *Geschichte* and the historicity of man *(Geschichtlichkeit des Daseins)* and there is above all the eschatological event.

It is no accident that one of Bultmann's major works should be called *History and Eschatology* or that the collection of his sermons should bear the title *This World and the Beyond.* He is constantly concerned with the fact that man lives in tension between the world of nature and history and that of *Geschichte* and eschatological event. It is not that a man flees the one for the other like a hermit seeking peace in his lonely cell but, rather, that man as a historical being-in-the-world must encounter history as *Geschichte* and can encounter the eschatological event. In other words, he must be challenged by those things of which the New Testament and the church speak in their mythical language. This is of course especially the case for Bultmann, since he is convinced that only the proclamation of those matters of which the New Testament and the church speak can offer a man authentic existence in the world.

This is the task to which he directs himself in demythologizing. Recognizing that the events of which the New Testament and the church speak are couched in language unintelligible to modern man—in the language of myth as he defines it—then he seeks for a way to express the intention of that language in nonmythological terms, to *de*mythologize it, or better, to interpret it existentially.

If we ask what the purpose of myth is, what the intention of mythological language is, then the answer runs: "Man's understanding of himself."[7] "Myth speaks of the power or the powers which man supposes he experiences as the ground and limit of his world and of his own activity and suffering. He describes these powers in terms derived from the visible world. . . . He speaks of the other world in terms of this world, and of the gods in terms derived from human life."[8] In other words, myth expresses man's understanding of his existence in the world, his self-understanding, and insofar as this existence is believed to owe its origin, form and possibilities to powers beyond man, which is uniformly the case in the ancient world and certainly so in the New Testament and the church, then those powers are depicted in worldly and human terms. Myth then objectifies man's self-understanding or, more accurately, it objectifies the nonobjective powers which are regarded as ultimately controlling man's existence in the world, and it does this because it uses objectifying, mythical imagery to describe them and their power. The problem with this objectifying imagery is that it is clumsy and ultimately inappropriate to its subject matter. So the problem is not only that to take myth literally is to misunderstand its true function but also that even when that function is properly understood the objectifying imagery can be a hindrance rather than a help. "The real purpose of myth is to speak of a transcendent power which controls the world and man, but that purpose is impeded and obscured by the terms in which it is expressed."[9] So we are faced with a document, the New Testament, which has a message concerning man's existence in the world that is crucial to the existence of any and every man in the world. But this message is couched in terms of objectifying, mythical imagery, which is not only unacceptable to men in the world today; it is not even the best way of expressing that message.

Bultmann's proposal to demythologize the message of the New Testament and the church concerning man's existence in the world is essentially a proposal to find another way to express that message than by the use of mythical imagery. It is essential to recognize the fact that he has *two* criticisms of that imagery. The first is, as we noted earlier, that it usually involves something which is simply ridiculous to modern man—a three-story universe with clouds as celestial elevators, for example, or evil spirits causing illness and being exorcised by incantations. The second and more important criticism is that the imagery involved in myth is ultimately inappropriate to the subject matter and so hinders rather than helps the message. This latter point has to be stressed, because it is the point at which Bultmann's demythologizing program must be tested. One can raise questions about his understanding of myth and still not have scratched the surface of his program. The real questions arise in connection with the claim that the use of New Testament mythology is not in fact today the most effective and appropriate way of expressing the New Testament message, and that Bultmann himself has found a better way. Bultmann's better way is to use the categories of existentialist philosophy to express that which in the New Testament is expressed by the use of myth. The message of the New Testament is that man is in bondage to demonic powers and that God has acted to redeem him from these forever. Our task is to produce an existentialist interpretation of this mythical language. But in effect this is what Bultmann has been doing ever since he encountered Heidegger in the 1920s. He had always accepted the New Testament as normative for his theology and after his encounter with Heidegger he had consciously sought to use that existentialist philosophy in his explication of the theology of that New Testament. So in his demythologizing program Bultmann actually recapitulated the basic thrusts of his own theological position, which is the reason why a debate about demythologizing can rapidly become a debate about the Bultmannian theology.

In his initial essay, "New Testament and Mythology," Bultmann offers a description of "Demythologizing in Outline,"[10] and here we find that he begins with "Human Existence Apart from Faith." This is inauthentic existence, the existence in which a man has based his life on the tangible and visible and so becomes the prisoner and slave of corruption, wholly incapable of achieving authenticity. In contrast to this, there is authentic existence, "The Life of Faith," in which man finds himself set free from the bondage of his past and living in the spirit of the "as though not" of I Corinthians 7:29-31. "Outwardly everything remains as before, but inwardly his relation to the world has been radically changed."[11]

This transition to authentic existence is made possible by "The Event of Redemption." Bultmann argues at some length that although philosophy can describe authentic existence so far as faith is concerned, only God can make it possible and that the message of the New Testament and the church is that he has done so in "The Event of Jesus Christ." This "event" is the cross, a historical event which acquires cosmic dimensions; it is "not just an event of the past which can be contemplated, but is the eschatological event in and beyond time insofar as it is . . . an ever-present reality."[12]

The cross is ever present in the kerygma of the church and this is the meaning of the mythical event of the resurrection. The cross and resurrection "form a single, indivisible cosmic event,"[13] although the one is ultimately historical and the other mythical. The meaning of the myth of the resurrection is that the cross is efficacious—"*faith in the resurrection is really the same thing as faith in the saving efficacy of the cross*"[14] —and the cross becomes efficacious by being present to the hearer in the kerygma: "Christ meets us in the preaching as one crucified and risen. He meets us in the word of preaching and nowhere else. The faith of Easter is just this— faith in the word of preaching."[15] Later, Bultmann was to agree to accept a description of his interpretation of the resurrection as "Jesus has risen in the kerygma."[16]

It can, of course, be claimed that to speak of an eschatological act of God is still to use the language of mythology; however, in a short but most important "conclusion" to his demythologizing proposal Bultmann denies this. He denies it because (1) it does not use the traditional mythological imagery which is unacceptable to modern man and so "is not mythology in the traditional sense," and (2) the act referred to "is not a miraculous supernatural event, but an historical event in time and space."[17] This remains always for Bultmann the central paradox which he will never give up. There is a historical event, the cross, which becomes the eschatological act of God—the means whereby the one who determines human existence makes authentic existence possible—as it becomes present to man as address in the kerygma. This is the stumbling block (*skandalon*) "which will not be removed by philosophical discussion but only by faith and obedience." It is immune from proof and "it is precisely its immunity from proof which secures the Christian proclamation from the charge of being mythological."[18]

Demythologizing is ultimately an existentialist interpretation of the New Testament, the documents of faith, and since Bultmann is predominantly an interpreter of the New Testament it may be appropriate to conclude our descriptive discussion of his theology by saying a few words about this. Any historical document has to be read with a certain "pre-understanding" if it is to say anything to us. We must approach it from a certain perspective, have certain questions in our mind to ask of it. This is as true of the New Testament as of any other historical document. We can approach it from the perspective of an interest in the social history of the Roman Empire, or in the popular Hellenistic philosophies of the first century, or in the development of Greek language in contact with a predominantly Semitic culture, and in each case it will have different things to say to us. Each of these "perspectives" Bultmann would call a "pre-understanding" and he would also say that a pre-understanding need not necessarily be as explicit or conscious as it is in these examples. Without a pre-understanding the texts would have no meaning for us; we cannot interpret a text until we have found the perspective to which it speaks, until we have framed questions which it can answer. So the question is not whether we should approach a text with a pre-understanding—that is inevitable—but what pre-understanding is proper in the case of any given text.

In the case of the Bible there can be only one answer: the question with which to come to the Bible is the question of human existence. I am driven to the Bible "by the urge to inquire existentially about my own existence."[19] This is true not only of the Bible but of all historical texts, "for the ultimate purpose in the study of history is to realize consciously the possibilities it affords for the understanding of human existence."[20] So all historical texts, including the Bible, are to be approached in light of the question of human existence, and this means, for Bultmann, in light of the question of human existence as this is explicated in existentialist analysis of that existence. In other words, these texts are to be approached with an existentialist pre-understanding.

Approached in this way all historical texts offer us possibilities for the understanding of human existence; each can challenge us at the level of our understanding of our own existence; but only the Bible can become the word which addresses me personally with the possibility of a transition to authentic existence.

# VIII
# Retrospect and Prospect: The Promise of Bultmann

One of the most notable things about the Bultmannian theology has been the controversy which it has aroused, and one of Bultmann's own particular characteristics is his readiness to enter into debate. The result is that there is now a very considerable amount of literature about Bultmann, and no small amount of literature in which Bultmann is in debate with his critics. Our purpose here is to present what we would regard as the main strength of Bultmann's theological position and, in doing so, to take note of some of the criticisms that have been made of that position and to attempt to assess their significance.

It is perhaps important to begin by calling attention again to the fact that Bultmann is self-consciously a Lutheran theologian. He explicitly claims this; for example, in his demythologizing program he considers himself to be standing in succession to Paul and to Luther:

> Our radical attempt to demythologize the New Testament is in fact a perfect parallel to St. Paul's and Luther's doctrine of justification by faith alone apart from the works of the Law . . . . it destroys every false security and every false demand for it on the part of man. . . . The man who wishes to believe in God as his God must realize that he has nothing in his hand on which to base his faith. He is suspended in mid-air, and cannot demand a proof of the Word that addresses him.[1]

For Bultmann, then, the attempt to ground faith in a historical event—apart from the sheer factuality of the cross itself—is not only wrong but wrong-headed. It breaks down on the theological ground that it would no longer be "justification by faith alone," and it breaks down also on the practical ground that history cannot in fact give the kind of evidence for which faith asks. "Similarly, the framework of nature and history is profane and it is only in the light of the word of proclamation that nature and history become for the believer, contrary to all appearances, the field of the divine activity."[2] Nothing could be more characteristic of Bultmann than this combination of a self-conscious affirmation of a fundamental principle of a particular Christian tradition with an acceptance of the radical secularity of the world "of nature and history." It is here that his greatness lies: in the way in which he has succeeded in holding fast to the essentials of a deeply theological tradition while accepting a radically secular view of the world. It is my opinion that his critics have failed to match him at this point: either they have abandoned some aspect of the former or they have failed to come to grips with the latter. Of course, it is also true that they have for the most part not wanted to match him at this point!

Let us consider, first, the place of man in the world of nature and of history. In the biblical view the world was the center of the universe and everything else revolved around it. It had been created a comparatively short time ago, within a period of time readily imaginable by people accustomed to counting time by generations, and man himself was created shortly thereafter. The world had been created for man and the whole history of that world, and of the universe of which it is the center, was rapidly moving to a climax in which the destiny of man would be resolved. Under these conditions it was natural to think of man being confronted by God in the world of nature and history because the whole thing was sufficiently small for a man to think it natural that he should be confronted within it by the power who ruled it and was responsible for it.

Today, however, all that has changed. We now know that the world is an obscure planet making up part of one solar system among billions of solar systems which in turn make up one galaxy among billions of galaxies. It came into existence, we know not how, a period of time ago which we find it almost impossible to imagine. As for the universe itself, it may well be that that has always existed; certainly time, as conceived by man, has as little relevance in thinking about it as does distance, conceived in terms of the world and the sun, in attempting to measure it. Man himself is a comparative latecomer on the world and his total historical existence, say ten thousand years, is very little in comparison with that of his prehistoric yet recognizably human antecedents, say one million years. In turn that is almost as nothing in comparison with the age of the earth itself and that, in its turn, is absolutely as nothing compared to the age of the universe, if, indeed, the universe is not in fact literally ageless. As for the history of man in the world, if man himself does not bring it to an end with a bang of his own making, then it will simply whimper out over an unimaginable sequence of time and events as the world gradually loses its power to sustain life. With this kind of a picture it is extraordinarily difficult to think of man being confronted in history by the power responsible for all things.

It is here that Bultmann comes into his own, for what he does, in effect, is to recognize that despite all the unimaginable elements that go to make up the history of man in the world and of the world in the universe, each man has a concrete, limited and very real personal history. Then, he claims, God is known as the one who determines this history. Bultmann is often accused of dissolving the history of man into the historicity of the individual, but it would be better to recognize that it is the development of human knowledge which is dissolving the history of man—in the sense that that history is central to the cosmos and therefore the natural overriding concern to the power who rules the cosmos—and it is Bultmann who is rescuing for us a history of man in terms of which the biblical categories still have some relevance. It would be better still to say that as human knowledge progresses we learn the better to appreciate the essential nature of human history in the world and so to grasp the relevance of the biblical message and to build our theology accordingly. This is what Bultmann is doing and it is hard to imagine a way of doing it more relevant to the reality of man, the world and the universe as we are being forced to recognize it today.

Now let us turn, second, to the idea of acts of God in history. In the biblical view this was a comparatively simple matter. God had created the world as the center of the universe an imaginable number of generations ago and would bring it to an end, to be replaced by something different and better, within the readily foreseeable future. In the past he had reached down into the history of the world to effect the events crucial to the salvation of man: the deliverance from Egypt, the raising of David to kingship, the sending of Jesus, and so on. The history of man in the world was a kind of battleground for good and evil forces, both of which could effectively control both men and nature, and man hoped for the imminent victory of the good. So imminent and concrete was the hope for God's final intervention in history that in the first century Jews repeatedly began armed revolts against Rome in the expectation that God would end them in the victory that would transform the world, and Christians in Thessalonica stopped working because they believed that the end would come before they had need to restock their larders!

Here, again, everything has changed, and it is the greatness of Bultmann that he has recognized this change and taken it seriously. The Jews were defeated in their revolts against Rome, and the Christians in Thessalonica would have starved to death had it not been for the charity of their brethren or the persuasion of the apostle Paul to go back to work. But more than this, we have learned that in human history every event has an effective and sufficient cause that can be explained in purely historical terms. The extent of our knowledge of history is limited, and historical knowledge is always to some degree ambiguous, but there is no such thing at the level of world history as events which cannot be known by scientific historical knowledge, or events which do not have sufficient causes which can be understood in terms of such knowledge. There may be things we do not know with certainty, or which we do not understand, because our methods are not yet sufficient or because we lack the necessary sources, but to put "God" in those places would be to follow the example of American cartographers in the early nineteenth century who regularly depicted the "River of the West" in the blank space now filled in by the Great Basin![3]

At this point we should perhaps pause a moment to make an aside which we hope will avoid possible confusion. Earlier, when we were discussing the possibility of historical knowledge providing support for faith (see above, pp. 33–36), we claimed that this was not possible because such knowledge was too relative and ambiguous. But now are we not claiming that, for all its relativity and ambiguity, historical knowledge is sufficient to rule out the idea of an act of God in history? And if we do claim this, is not this a case of "heads I win, tails you lose"? No, not quite! The crux of the matter is that although historical knowledge is more or less relative and ambiguous in the case of any given event, the totality of our knowledge of various sequences of events—the American Civil War, for example, or the exploration of the American west— is more than sufficient to rule out the idea of an event which breaks the historical sequence of cause and effect and has therefore to be ascribed to a power not subject to the laws of history.

To return to our main point: it follows from what we have said that God cannot be the effective cause of an event within history; only a man or a people's faith in God can be that. Moreover, since the process of history is uniform and not random—if it were random any kind of historical existence would become impossible—then it follows that there never has been and there never will be an event within history (that is, world history) of which God has been or will be the effective cause. Many people shrink from this conclusion and perhaps most Christians and Jews would do so. But Bultmann does not shrink from it. It has been argued against him, of course, that there are " 'mighty deeds of God' which have happened and will happen,"[4] that "it is necessary to point to the objectively real character of the object of faith,"[5] that there are "saving historical facts which the Bible recounts . . . [and which] have really happened in our world."[6] But to a practicing historian such statements are only confusing. That a Semitic tribe or tribes escaped from bondage in ancient Egypt, that a Jesus bar Joseph from Nazareth was crucified by the Romans as a messianic pretender, these are the things which a historian knows. But that these are "mighty deeds of God" he can never know. To the historian they are deeds of people, motivated by hopes and fears, under economic and political pressure, but still people and not God. So long as history means "that history which historians investigate" God can never be visible in it.

Bultmann, himself a first-class practicing historian, knows this very well and is fully prepared to reckon with its consequences. For him God is not known at the level of "that history which historians investigate," i.e., what we called earlier "history as *Historie*," but at the level of "history as *Geschichte*" and especially at the level of "the historicity of man." That God is known at these levels is the testimony of faith, and that men have believed this and changed the course of that history which historians investigate because they believed it is the testimony of any practicing historian.

Bultmann's greatest strength lies in the way in which he has fearlessly accepted the challenge of the modern view of the world and its history and worked out a theology which takes that view with the seriousness it deserves. We say "worked out a theology" but we could equally well say "interpreted biblical categories," for these are one and the same thing for him. But for all that Bultmann has taken the modern view of the world and its history seriously, he has not abandoned the particularity of Christian faith. Although he is fully prepared to interpret the Bible in light of a modern viewpoint he is not prepared to abandon it for that viewpoint, and the way in which he resolves his dilemma at this point is perhaps the most remarkable thing about his theology. We may approach this matter from the standpoint of a consideration of the concept of "salvation history."

We may say that the Bible presents to us the history of God's dealings with man, a history we may call "salvation history" following the German practice of using *Heilsgeschichte* in this context. Roughly this salvation history may be said to encompass at least the following: the creation and fall of man; the foundation of the Jewish people, the people of God, their captivity in Egypt and their deliverance from Egypt; the giving of the Law and the entry into Canaan; the coming of King David and the prophets; the coming of Jesus as the Messiah, Son of David, and his ministry, cross and resurrection; and the formation of the new People of God, the Christian church. It is expected that this history will soon reach its climax with the return of Jesus as Son of man and the establishment of the full salvation of man. The Bible sees all this on one plane; it thinks of it as one coherent, continuous and all-encompassing history. But we can no longer do that, for as we reflect upon this history it becomes evident that we have here a whole mixture of different kinds of things. In the first place we have aspects of worldly history, history as *Historie:* there was a Semitic tribe or tribes which escaped from Egypt; King David is as historical an individual as Abraham Lincoln; Jesus is known to Roman history; and so on. Then we have history reflected upon in the light of religious faith and so "acquiring cosmic dimensions" as Bultmann would put it: over a period of centuries of confessional reflection and recital a folk memory of an escape from captivity becomes the Exodus narrative; over decades of similar liturgical reflection and confession the memory of the crucifixion of Jesus becomes the Passion narrative; and so on. This we may call history as *Geschichte*. Then we also have myths: the creation and fall, the resurrection and the coming on the clouds as Son of man, and many others. We could go on enumerating other categories of material, legend for example, or saga, but we have said enough to make the point: from a modern viewpoint, salvation history is not a coherent concept.

Bultmann sees this clearly and what he does in effect is to ask himself if there is not an essential here which can be grasped and interpreted in terms that would be real to a modern viewpoint. As he sees it the essential is in fact twofold. To be true to the biblical insight there must be something out there at the level of world history which forms the basis for the salvation history. At the same time, if we are to be true to the modern viewpoint this something must make its impact upon the individual at the level of his historicity: "only an occurrence that is experienced and laid hold of in faith could be designated as the salvation-occurrence or as the history of salvation."[7] This "something" is the cross of Jesus, the event that is at one and the same time historical and eschatological. As a historical event it is as relative and ambiguous as any other and for this reason Bultmann is completely uninterested in historical information about it. Information as to *how* Jesus died—nobly or badly, with confidence in God or railing against his fate—would be historical information that could change tomorrow, and it would also serve only to put Jesus in a general category with other men who died for a belief. There is nothing here that could be significant for faith. The only thing significant for faith at the level of world history is *that* Jesus died. What makes the cross significant for faith, and an occurrence in salvation history, is that it is also the eschatological event and that God encounters man through it as it is represented as eschatological event in the kerygma.

In this way Bultmann achieves his goal of being true to the biblical insight and at the same time taking a responsible attitude to a modern view of the things concerned. Again here it is very difficult to fault him. There have been many attempts to argue that the kerygma requires more history than simply the historical factuality of Jesus and his cross; but these arguments all run aground on the hard rock of the fact that such knowledge would be relative and ambiguous, and it is difficult to see, therefore, how much help it would be at the level of faith. It is sometimes said that faith must know at least that Jesus realized the potential for authentic existence. But it is hard to see how this could ever be historical knowledge. It is difficult to judge the quality of the existence even of one's friends and contemporaries, and the difficulty reaches practically to impossibility in the case of figures from the past. Perhaps in cases where we have extensive records, including autobiographical records, we could hope to do so. But in the case of Jesus our records are second hand and fragmentary; moreover, they have been shaped and reshaped by the faith of the early church, so any such knowledge of the quality of Jesus' existence is beyond our reach. The real point, however, is not that such knowledge of Jesus is difficult to attain or even impossible, it is that such knowledge would do nothing more than put Jesus in a category with other good and noble men. Even if Jesus were demonstrably the best and noblest of them all, this would still have nothing to say to the claim that through him God has wrought the salvation of man—that Jesus Christ is God's eschatological act, as Bultmann likes to put it.

From the opposite standpoint Bultmann has been reproached for maintaining the one link with world history, the factuality of the cross. The most important names here are those of Karl Jaspers and Schubert Ogden.[8] Jaspers sees Jesus as a paradigmatic individual, one among several whose "overcoming of all human rigidities and presumptions" represents a "breakthrough to truthfulness and love that knows no bounds," and who represents, therefore, that "which the philosopher seeks."[9] But there is no necessary link here with the factuality of the cross. Ogden regards Jesus as the "decisive" revelation of the primordial love of God but argues that this love is also revealed elsewhere, and that authentic existence is a possibility in fact to the man who responds to this love wherever it meets him. There is no *necessary* link between Jesus and a man's realization of authentic existence.[10] Both Jaspers and Ogden recognize the "fallen" state of man, that is, that man cannot of himself and by himself achieve authentic existence, but they refuse to concede that the "transcendence" (Jaspers) or the "primordial love of God" (Ogden) which makes this possible is necessarily linked to the historical Jesus in any way, even though in fact it may be so for many who stand in the Western tradition. Jesus may be the best or even decisive example of what makes authentic existence possible, but he is not the only way to that existence.

Bultmann's reply to both men is essentially the same: You have failed to recognize the essential stumbling block (*skandalon*) of Christian faith. This essential link between Jesus and his cross and the proclamation by means of which alone authentic existence is made possible is what the New Testament calls the *skandalon*; it is a true insight of New Testament faith, and it is for theology to explicate it and not to deny it. One can accuse Bultmann of being "illiberal" or "inconsistent" in maintaining this point, but it must be recognized that he is being true to the tradition he self-consciously represents. It may be a moot point whether a position such as Jaspers' or Ogden's could be justified on the basis of the New Testament, but it is quite impossible that it could be on the basis of the New Testament as interpreted in the Lutheran tradition.

The aspect of Bultmann's theology which has been most strenuously discussed by those closest to him, and especially by his own pupils, is the "question of the historical Jesus," which, as we pointed out earlier, is really two questions: the related questions of the relationship between the historical Jesus and the kerygma, and of the significance of the historical Jesus for Christian faith. For Bultmann, Jesus is not a Christian. In *Primitive Christianity* he is discussed in the section of the book dealing with Judaism, not Christianity, and the *Theology of the New Testament* begins with a sentence which became famous: "The message of Jesus is a presupposition for the theology of the New Testament rather than a part of that theology itself."[11]

A clear statement of Bultmann's position on this point is to be found in his 1936 essay, "Jesus and Paul," now in *Existence and Faith*[12] Here Jesus is presented as proclaiming the imminent eschatological event, the Reign of God, and as demanding a decision of men in response to the challenge of his proclamation. "But . . . the decision to which he summons men by his proclamation is the definitive decision . . . that insofar as anyone hears his word, God's salvation is now freely offered to him."[13] So we have the rather strange position being taken that although for Jesus the eschatological act of God was still in the future, albeit imminent and already breaking-in, response to the challenge of his message could lead to "salvation," i.e., to authentic existence. For Paul, on the other hand, Jesus himself was the eschatological act of God, he was God's Messiah, and his cross and resurrection mean that "now is the day of salvation!" (II Cor. 6:2). This is the real difference between Paul and Jesus.

"Jesus looks to the future and points his hearers to the *coming* Reign of God, which, to be sure, is coming even now, is already breaking in. Paul, on the other hand, looks back and points to what has already occurred. For him the turn of the age has already taken place, the day of salvation is already present!"[14]

Bultmann is always consistent on these points. Whatever the message of Jesus made possible for his hearers, so far as we are concerned it is the eschatological act of God in the cross and the kerygma which alone makes authentic existence possible. So Christian faith begins with the cross and kerygma, and the Easter faith is faith that Jesus is risen in the kerygma. The discussion of various aspects of this position has been extensive and vigorous and has led to the development of characteristically "post-Bultmannian" theological positions. A review of the details of the discussion and of the "post-Bultmannian" theological positions it has produced lies beyond the scope of this book,[15] but the main issues must be mentioned.

The first question that has been raised is that of whether Bultmann's understanding of the lack of any real material relationship between the historical Jesus and the kerygma does justice to the New Testament itself. True, it is in accordance with what we find in Paul and John, but if we take up the Synoptic Gospels (Matthew, Mark and Luke) the situation changes somewhat. These Gospels proclaim the post-Easter kerygma as vigorously as any Epistle of Paul or the Gospel of John but they do so in the form of historicizing narratives; they are, in fact, a strange mixture of kerygma and history. Moreover, it has been argued, if we take up the matter of the historical Jesus himself we find that he had already shattered the categories of the ancient Judaism to which Bultmann assigns him. In his eschatological proclamation and in his challenge to the decision which made possible the transition to authentic existence he had already broken decisively with Jewish legalistic structures, and had already implied such christological claims that to acknowledge him as Messiah is the only possible response.[16]

Bultmann's reply to this was twofold.[17] In regard to the Synoptic Gospels he denies that there is any objective history in them and he claims that attempts to reconstruct such history from them always break down at the crucial point of knowledge as to how Jesus understood his own death. This is crucial because of the central role of the cross in the kerygma. If historical knowledge were essential to the kerygma then it would include knowledge of this point. But since in fact historical knowledge breaks down at this point, the gulf between historical knowledge of Jesus and the kerygma is both deep and wide. What the Synoptic Gospels do is not to offer us history in order to legitimate the kerygma but, rather, the opposite: they legitimate the history of Jesus as messianic history by viewing it in light of the kerygmatic

Christology! In regard to the message of Jesus and its implied christological claims, Bultmann agreed at once that Jesus was, in effect, an "eschatological phenomenon," that he did offer his hearers the challenge to authentic existence, and that this implied a Christology. But what did this mean? It meant that we could understand now the fact of the historical continuity between Jesus and the kerygma. It became intelligible to us why the kerygma should speak of Jesus as it did, when we knew how Jesus himself had spoken. But the kerygma never simply repeated Jesus' message. It spoke of him as he had spoken of the Reign of God, and in so doing it made the "once" of Jesus' message and ministry the "once-for-all" of the kerygma. Jesus could offer the challenge only to his hearers in his own day; the kerygma challenges any man in any day. The Proclaimer *had* to become the Proclaimed in order for this to happen and we must take this fact with full seriousness.

It is in this particular aspect of the discussion that we can see the necessity for more work and thought on the issues raised. Bultmann is right to protest against the idea of historical information legitimating the kerygma and he is right, further, in claiming that if the Synoptic Gospels legitimate anything, it is the history of Jesus as messianic history that is being legitimated. But this talk of "legitimation" is altogether too hasty. The question is much more that of what the nature of the Synoptic Gospels implies regarding the historical Jesus, the kerygma and the relationship between the two, and the problem is that our understanding of these Gospels is as yet in its infancy. We need a generation of work on them in light of the question raised by the discussion of the Bultmannian theology before we can go much further. Such work must be undertaken because Bultmann does build his theological viewpoint so strongly on Paul and John, to all intent and purpose ignoring the Synoptic Gospels. But the Synoptic Gospels are too considerable a part of the New Testament to be ignored in this way. Fortunately the rise of redaction criticism is guaranteeing that such work will be done.[18]

The fact that the message of Jesus can be interpreted existentially as making possible the transition to authentic existence for his hearers, and that the kerygma of the church is interpreted in exactly the same way in the Bultmannian theology, clearly holds out all kinds of possibilities for discussion and development. We shall concern ourselves with two that have been realized in particular and that are associated with the names of James M. Robinson and Herbert Braun.

James M. Robinson's *New Quest of the Historical Jesus* explored these parallels between the message of Jesus and the kerygma and then took up the existentialist understanding of history which Bultmann himself espouses, by means of which an encounter with the past at the level of self-understanding is mediated. This encounter with Jesus and his offer of the challenge to true self-understanding is, then, precisely parallel to the encounter with Christ as eschatological event mediated by the kerygma, and we have therefore a double access to Jesus and to the authentic existence he alone can offer. This "new quest" of the historical Jesus was sharply criticized by Bultmann on the grounds that it tended to render the kerygma unnecessary and hence was illegitimate. One should notice again Bultmann's instinctive appeal to the history of the matter as theologically significant: the Proclaimer *did* become the Proclaimed, so *had* to become the Proclaimed and so *must* become the Proclaimed. Robinson subsequently modified his position somewhat and the discussion continues.[19]

A further development out of the basic Bultmannian position is that of the "new hermeneutic" of Ernst Fuchs and Gerhard Ebeling.[20] This takes its point of departure in Bultmann's understanding of the kerygma as essentially an event, that is, as a proclamation in which God confronts man through the eschatological event. For Bultmann, as we have seen, it is very important that the kerygma should be understood as that word by means of which something "happens." What the "new hermeneutic" does, in effect, is to take up this idea and develop it into the concept of a "language event." In his later years Heidegger himself has tended to concern himself with the way in which reality is disclosed in language, an interest which can be characterized by the sentence: "Language is the house of being." The "new hermeneutic" fastens upon this idea—in the case of its American practitioners, upon related ideas drawn from the "secular" philosophers of language and literary critics[21] —and develops the concept of a reality which manifests itself in language, of a reality which "comes to word" in a "language event."

"Language event," then, is a phrase used to denote the concept of words having the power to effect something, to make something happen. In the case of the words which concern a theologian, what is effected is "faith," and so we can say that faith "comes to word in" the kerygma. This is another way of saying what Bultmann has always said, and in itself it is an interesting and promising development. It is especially promising in that it clearly intends—particularly in its American form—to turn for help to "secular" students of language as, in his day, Bultmann turned for help to a "secular" philosopher. One has the feeling that to start with the Bultmannian understanding of the kerygma as event, to develop this as language event, and to take serious account of nontheological work on language ought to prove a fruitful avenue of inquiry, and one awaits with real interest the results of the work that is being done here.[22]

Herbert Braun is the "post-Bultmannian" to whose work Bultmann himself has been most responsive. Braun moves in the direction pointed out by fact that there is a real parallel in the *effect* of the message of Jesus—namely, making possible the transition to authentic existence for the hearer—and the *effect* of the proclamation of the church.[23] Concerning himself with the message of Jesus, on the one hand, and various formulations by the early church, on the other, Braun explores the parallels. He argues that in the message of Jesus we have at one and the same time a radical demand for obedience and the proclamation of a radical acceptance by God which enables man to respond to the demand. In Paul the terminology changes so that we now have christological titles and claims for the person of Jesus and so on, but the essential theme remains the same. The concept of justification by faith and the consequent ethical demands express exactly the same understanding of the situation of a man before God as did the radical demand-acceptance theme in the message of Jesus. In the case of John the terminology changes again. Now we have the use of concepts from the Gnostic redeemer myth[24] to describe Jesus, and the imminent expectation of judgment characteristic of Jesus (at the coming of the Son of man) and Paul (at the coming of Jesus as Lord) has practically disappeared. But the claim that the believer now has "life" and the demands which this lays upon him as John presents it echo the same understanding of the situation of the believer before God. So through all the variables of Christology and expressions of the faith there is one constant: the way a man now is able to understand himself before God. As Bultmann puts it approvingly: "He [Braun] actually succeeds in demonstrating the material unity of the Christ-kerygma with the proclamation of Jesus. The constant is the self-understanding of the believer; the Christology is the variable."[25]

Encouraged no doubt by the reception given to his first essay, Braun returned to the theme in 1961 with a further essay, "The Problem of a New Testament Theology."[26] Here he turns to the problem created by the fact that the New Testament contains many disparate ideas and argues that these point to the still deeper problem of understanding God. "These diversities refer, for their part, to a still deeper problem within the New Testament statements, God as palpable and given and God as not palpable and not given. What is God finally in the New Testament sense?" The answer deserves quotation in full:

God then means much rather the whence of my being agitated. My being agitated, however, is determined by the "I may" and "I ought"; determined by being taken care of and by obligation. Being taken care of and obligation, however, do not approach me from the universe, but from another, from my fellow man. The word of proclamation and the act of love reach me—if they really do reach me—from my fellow man. God is the whence of my being taken care of and of my being obliged, which comes to me from my fellow man.[27]

As we had occasion to note in Chapter V, Bultmann fully approves such a statement. He would do so because it speaks of the reality of God but avoids what Bultmann would regard as the objectifying language of myth, using, rather, the language of human experience and obligation.

It is hoped that this brief review of some of the discussion of Bultmann's theological position and some of the developments from it may have helped the reader to grasp something of the contribution which Bultmann is making to the current theological scene. It remains now for me only to answer the question I asked at the beginning of this book: Is Bultmann the last great German Protestant theologian? The answer: He may well be, because it is difficult to see where one goes from him without abandoning something of the tradition he self-consciously represents. If one is to be true to the modern view of the world, one cannot build more history into the system than Bultmann does; if one is to be true to the particularity of Christian faith, one cannot abandon the one link with history in the cross. If one is to achieve relevance in communication, then demythologizing and that which Braun is attempting are clearly both legitimate and necessary.

# *Notes*

The following abbreviations are used for books by Bultmann or which contain essays by him. When no name is given, the reference is always to Bultmann himself. Publication details will be found in the Bibliography.

| | |
|---|---|
| CS | *Christian Scholar.* |
| EF | *Existence and Faith: Shorter Writings of Rudolf Bultmann.* Translated by Schubert M. Ogden. |
| GV | *Glauben und Verstehen.* |
| HE | *History and Eschatology: The Presence of Eternity.* |
| HJKC | *The Historical Jesus and the Kerygmatic Christ.* Eds. C. E. Braaten and R. E. Harrisville. |
| JCM | *Jesus Christ and Mythology.* |
| JThC, I | *The Bultmann School of Biblical Interpretation: New Directions?* J. M. Robinson *et al.* (*Journal for Theology and the Church,* Vol. I). |
| JThC, II | *Translating Theology into the Modern Age.* R. Bultmann *et al.* (*Journal for Theology and the Church,* Vol. II). |
| JThC, IV | *History and Hermeneutic.* W. Pannenberg *et al.* (*Journal for Theology and the Church,* Vol. IV). |
| JW | *Jesus and the Word.* |
| KM | *Kerygma and Myth.* |
| KM, II | *Kerygma and Myth,* Vol. II. |
| PC | *Primitive Christianity in Its Contemporary Setting.* |
| TNT, I, II | *Theology of the New Testament,* Vols. I and II. |

## Chapter I. Introduction

1. We include Swiss-German under the rubric "German"!

2. John B. Cobb, Jr., *Living Options in Protestant Theology* (Philadelphia. Westminster Press, 1962), p. 258.

3. *Ibid.*, p. 284, points out that the only other men of comparable theological influence in America who were similarly not systematic theologians or philosophers of religion are the Niebuhr brothers, H. Richard and Reinhold, both of whom were professors of Christian social ethics.

4. In the Bibliography we shall speak of Bultmann's technical achievements in the field of New Testament scholarship.

5. These include Romans, I and II Corinthians, Galatians, Philippians, I Thessalonians and Philemon. *EF,* p. 111.

6. In contrast to his position on the Epistles of Paul, Bultmann does not concern himself with the question of the authenticity of the Epistles of John, that is with the question as to whether they come from the same author as the Gospel of John. *TNT,* II, 3. The reason for this is that they express the same view of Christian faith as does the Gospel, something that Bultmann would hold is not the case with the Epistles that are ascribed to Paul, but are not from his hand, for example, Colossians, Ephesians, I and II Timothy, Titus. The crux of the matter is the view of Christian faith to which expression is being given.

7. *TNT,* II, 237. On Bultmann's understanding of the nature and task of theology and its relationship to faith, see the discussion in Chapter V.

## Chapter II. Life, Times and Work of Rudolf Bultmann

1. A good account of both Barth's and Bultmann's theological education is to be found in James D. Smart, *The Divided Mind of Modern Theology* (Philadelphia: Westminster Press, 1967).

2. Doctor-father: the professor who guides a student through his doctoral dissertation. In Germany this relationship is usually a very close and personal one.

3. On Weiss and the revolution he started, see N. Perrin, *The Kingdom of God in the Teaching of Jesus* (Philadelphia. Westminster Press, 1963).

4. *PC,* p. 86.

5. Smart, *Divided Mind,* pp. 33-36 *et passim.*

6. *Ibid.,* p. 36.

7. Bultmann, "Autobiographical Reflections," in C. W. Kegley (ed.) *The Theology of Rudolf Bultmann* (New York: Harper & Row, 1966), p. xxii.

8. See especially his "The Task of Theology in the Present Situation," *EF,* pp. 158-65, remarks originally addressed to his students at the opening of the spring semester in 1933.

9. *EF,* p. 288.

## Chapter III. Theology, Faith, and Authentic Existence

1. *GV,* I, 2.

2. *EF,* p. 93.

3. John B. Cobb, Jr., *Living Options in Protestant Theology*, p. 227.

4. *CS*, 43 (1960), 213-14.

5. *Ibid.*, 218-19.

6. *JThC*, II (1965), 94.

7. See particularly the discussion in *TNT*, II, 237-39.

8. In connection with what follows, we would call attention to the careful and illuminating comparison of Heidegger and Bultmann carried out by John Macquarrie, *An Existentialist Theology* (Harper Torchbook No. 125; New York: Harper & Row, 1965).

9. Macquarrie, *An Existentialist Theology*, p. 113.

10. *Ibid.*, p. 117.

11. *Ibid.*, p. 136.

12. *JCM*, p. 56.

13. *Ibid.*, p. 74.

14. *Ibid.*, pp. 74f.

15. *Ibid.*, pp. 74f., italics supplied.

16. *KM*, I, 17.

17. *EF*, p. 95.

18. *Ibid.*, p. 107.

19. *JCM*, p. 76.

## Chapter IV. History, the Historicity of Man, and Eschatology

1. *JCM*, pp. 15-16. By "spiritual powers" I would take Bultmann to mean such things as the influence which led to Luther's faith in God, to Alexander's faith in the destiny of Greek culture, and Napoleon's in the future of revolutionary France.

2. *EF*, pp. 103ff.

3. *HE*, p. 151.

## Chapter V. God, Jesus and History

1. *GV*, I, 1-25.

2. A. Harnack, *What Is Christianity?* (Harper Torchbooks No. 17; New York: Harper & Row, 1957), pp. 37, 38.

3. "... religion may be called the soul of morality and morality the soul of religion." Harnack, *op. cit;* p. 73.

4. Harnack, *op. cit.*, p. 74.

5. For the story of the half century of discussion of Schweitzer's views, see N. Perrin, *The Kingdom of God in the Teaching of Jesus* (Philadelphia: Westminster Press, 1963).

6. Translation and discussion by C. A. Braaten (Philadelphia: Fortress Press, 1964). See also C. A. Braaten, "Martin Kähler on the Historic, Biblical Christ," *HJKC*, pp. 79-105.

7. For a discussion of Kähler and Bultmann's relationship to him, see N. Perrin, *Rediscovering the Teaching of Jesus (New York: Harper & Row, 1967), pp. 216-23.*

8. *GV*, I, 2.

9. *Ibid.*, pp. 2-13. The reader will recognize the echoes of matters discussed in Chapter IV.

10. We are not giving the whole of his argument, but only some of the characteristic elements from it to illustrate our point.

11. *GV*, I, 18.

12. *Ibid.*, pp. 19-24.

13. On this aspect of Bultmann's theology see Schubert Ogden, "Introduction" in *EF*, especially pp. 14ff.

14. *GV*, I, 26-37. English translation in *Christian Scholar*, 43 (1960), 213-222.

15. *JThC*, II (1965), 83-95.

16. *Christian Scholar;* 43 (1960), 216.

17. *JThC*, II (1965), 94, Bultmann's italics.

18. *GV*, I, 11.

19. For the modern quest for a scholarly methodology for reconstructing the teaching of Jesus and Bultmann's part in it, see N. Perrin, *Rediscovering the Teaching of Jesus*, Chapter I.

20. *JW*, p. 11.

## Chapter VI. The Kerygma, Faith and Self-Understanding

1. *TNT*, II, 239, Bultmann's italics.

2. *Ibid.*

3. *EF*, p. 221.

4. *JCM*, p. 76, italics supplied.

5. *EF*, pp. 104-10.

6. *GV*, I, 229-44.

7. A very helpful discussion of this aspect of Heidegger's thought will be found in J. Macquarrie, *An Existentialist Theology*, pp. 194f.

8. *JThC*, IV, 153-54.

9. *KM*, p. 32.

10. The concept of "eschatological event" was discussed in Chapter IV.

11. *KM*, p. 36.

12. *Ibid.*, pp. 36-37.
13. *Ibid.*, p. 36.
14. *HJKC,* p. 41.
15. *JThC,* IV, 154.
16. *EF,* pp. 248-66.
17. *Ibid.*, p. 253.
18. *Ibid.*
19. *Ibid.*, p. 254.
20. *Ibid.*, p. 255. This is a good example of Bultmann's demythologizing, a subject which will concern us later.
21. *Ibid.*
22. *Ibid.*
23. Bultmann accepts the authenticity of a saying such as Luke 12:8f., and argues that Jesus proclaimed the coming of a heavenly figure, the Son of man, with whom, however, he did not identify himself.
24. *EF,* p. 20.
25. *Ibid.*, p. 260.
26. The version *simul iustus, simul peccator* is also found, with the same meaning. Both go back to Martin Luther.
27. *HE,* p. 154.

## Chapter VII. Demythologizing and the Existential Interpretation of the Documents of Faith

1. *KM,* p. 201.
2. *Ibid.*, p. 206.
3. *Ibid.*, p. 207.
4. *Ibid.*
5. *Ibid.*
6. *Ibid.*, pp. 7-8.
7. *Ibid.*, p. 10. The reference is, of course, to "man's understanding of himself" as this phrase is used in existentialist terminology to describe man's understanding of existence.
8. *Ibid.*
9. *Ibid.*, p. 11.
10. *Ibid.*, pp. 17-44.
11. *Ibid.*, p. 20.
12. *Ibid.*, p. 36.
13. *Ibid.*, p. 38.
14. *Ibid.*, p. 41, Bultmann's italics.

15. *Ibid.*
16. *HJKC*, p. 42.
17. *KM*, pp. 43-44.
18. *Ibid.*, p. 44.
19. *Ibid.*, p. 192.
20. *Ibid.*

## Chapter VIII. Retrospect and Prospect: The Promise of Bultmann

1. *KM*, pp. 210-11.
2. *Ibid.*, p. 201.
3. On this see Daniel J. Boorstin, *The Americans. The National Experience* (New York: Random House, 1965), pp. 223-27.
4. E. Ellwein, *KM*, p. 52.
5. E. Kinder, *KM*, p. 74.
6. *Ibid.*, p. 77.
7. *EF*, p. 233.
8. Ogden's criticism is in *Christ without Myth.* Bultmann replied to this by reviewing the book in the *Journal of Religion*, 42 (1962), 225-27. The Jaspers-Bultmann debate is now to be found in Karl Jaspers and Rudolf Bultmann, *Myth and Christianity*, trans. N. Gutermann (New York: Noonday Press, 1958). A discussion of this debate by H. W. Bartsch can be found in *Kerygma and Myth*, II.
9. Jaspers, *Myth and Christianity*, p. 82.
10. Ogden, *Christ without Myth*, Chapter IV.
11. *TNT*, I, 3.
12. *EF*, pp. 183-201.
13. *Ibid.*, pp. 194-95.
14. *EF*, p. 196.
15. Such a review is to be found in N. Perrin, *Rediscovering the Teaching of Jesus*, Chapter V.
16. Among others, these points are made by E. Käsemann and G. Bornkamm, both pupils of Bultmann. For the details of Käsemann's work, see Perrin, *Rediscovering*,, pp. 226ff. G. Bornkamm's views are in his *Jesus of Nazareth*, translated by Irene and Fraser McLuskey with James M. Robinson (New York: Harper & Row, 1960).
17. See his essay, "The Historical Jesus and the Kerygmatic Christ," *HJKC*, pp. 15-42.
18. On this see N. Perrin, *Redaction Criticism*, one volume in a three-volume series (*Literary Criticism, Form Criticism, Redaction*

*Criticism*) to be published in the fall of 1969 by Fortress Press, Philadelphia, under the editorship of Dan O. Via, Jr.

19. Further details and comments in Perrin, *Rediscovering,* pp. 229-33.

20. On this movement see especially J. M. Robinson and J. B. Cobb (eds.), *The New Hermeneutic* ("New Frontiers in Theology," No. 2. New York: Harper & Row, 1964). A major presentation of the viewpoint by an American theologian is R. W. Funk, *Language, Hermeneutic, and Word of God* (New York: Harper & Row, 1966).

21. See, for example, Funk, *Language,* Chapter IX.

22. I assume that the movement will move away from a rather special interest in the "question of the historical Jesus," which got it off to a bad start and for which Bultmann severely criticized it. No mention of this particular aspect of the matter has therefore been made in the text above. Details can be found in Perrin, *Rediscovering,* pp. 227-29.

23. H. Braun, "Der Sinn der neutestamentlichen Christologie," *Zeitschrift für Theologie und Kirche,* 54 (1957), 341-77. An English translation of this essay is promised for a future issue of *Journal for Theology and the Church.*

24. See the Bibliography for the Bultmannian use of this myth in interpreting the theology of John.

25. *HJKC,* p. 36.

26. Now in *JThC,* I (1965), 169-83.

27. Braun, *JThC,* I (1965), 182-83.

# *Bibliography*

## Works of More General Theological Interest

The following list is highly selective, and reflects a personal choice: the items below are simply those which have become most significant to me as I have sought to understand Bultmann as a New Testament scholar and as a theologian. And, because of the purpose for which this particular book has been written the preference has always been given to works available in English. All works are by Bultmann unless otherwise specified.

"Die liberale Theologie und die jüngste theologische Bewegung" ("Liberal Theology and the Most Recent Theological Movement") now to be found in R. Bultmann, *Glauben und Verstehen,* I (Tübingen: J. C. B. Mohr [Paul Siebeck], 1935,[5] 1964), 1-25. Originally published in 1924.

> This essay is discussed in some detail in Chapter V. It represents a reaction of Bultmann against liberal theology and his early sympathy for Karl Barth. He has also begun his acquaintance with Martin Heidegger. All in all, some of the characteristic Bultmannian emphases begin to appear here.

"What Sense Is There to Speak of God?" ("Welchen Sinn hat es, von Gott zu reden?"), trans. by F. H. Littel and to be found in *Christian Scholar,* 43 (1960), 213-22. Originally published in 1925.

> A characteristic statement of Bultmann's views of the relationship between God and the world and between God and human existence. We discuss these matters in Chapter V.

*Jesus and the Word,* trans. by L. C. Smith and E. H. Lantero (New York: Charles Scribner's Sons, 1934; paperback edition, 1958). Originally published as *Jesus* in 1926.

> One of the greatest historical treatments of Jesus ever to appear, this book reflects Bultmann's work on the tradition lying behind the Synoptic Gospels and also his particular understanding of history.

"The Concept of Revelation in the New Testament," trans. by Schubert M. Ogden in *Existence and Faith: Shorter Writings of Rudolf Bultmann,* selected, translated and introduced by Schubert M. Ogden ("Living Age Books" No. 29; New York: Meridian Books, 1960), pp. 58-91. Originally published in 1929. "The Historicity of Man and Faith," trans. by Schubert M. Ogden in *Existence and Faith,* pp. 92-110. Originally published in 1930.

These two articles represent first statements of major Bultmannian themes and are as important as anything he ever wrote for an understanding of his theological position.

"Das christliche Gebot der Nächstenliebe" (a trans., "To love your neighbor," reportedly in *The Scottish Periodical,* I [1947], 42-56, has been inaccessible to me), in *Glauben und Verstehen,* I, 229-44. Originally published in 1930.

An important essay for understanding Bultmann's approach to ethics.

"New Testament and Mythology," "A Reply to the Thesis of J. Schniewind," "Bultmann Replies to His Critics," trans. by R. H. Fuller in *Kerygma and Myth* (Harper Torchbook No. 80; New York: Harper & Row, 1961).

The first of these essays is Bultmann's original demythologizing proposal (made in 1941), the second and third are contributions by him to the subsequent debate. Demythologizing is the best known and most controversial of all Bultmann's theological proposals. We discuss it in Chapter VII.

"Man between the Times according to the New Testament," trans. by Schubert M. Ogden in *Existence and Faith,* pp. 248-66. Originally published in 1952.

A good statement of Bultmann's conception of the paradoxical nature of the Christian life and a characteristic example of his use of the "as though not" passage, I Corinthians 7:29-31, a use which, as Ogden himself correctly points out, is extremely frequent in Bultmann's writings.

*Theology of the New Testament,* I (1951), II (1955), trans. by K. Grobel (New York: Charles Scribner's Sons).

This two-volume work is one of Bultmann's major contributions to New Testament studies, since it is certainly the most important treatment of its subject to appear in many years. At the same time, Bultmann consciously stands theologically with Paul and John so his interpretation of their theologies is also a definitive statement of his own.

*This World and the Beyond,* trans. by H. Knight (New York: Charles Scribner's Sons, 1960).

A collection of sermons Bultmann preached in Marburg between 1936 and 1950.

*The Presence of Eternity: History and Eschatology* (New York: Harper & Row, 1957. Harper Torchbook No. 91, 1962 [as *History and Eschatology: The Presence of Eternity*]).

Originally written in English, these are the Gifford Lectures for 1955 and the definitive statement of Bultmann's understanding of history and eschatology carefully related by him to other contemporary understandings of history, particularly that of R. H. Collingwood.

*Jesus Christ and Mythology* (New York: Charles Scribner's Sons, 1958).

Perhaps the most useful short statement of some of Bultmann's characteristic views. The volume consists of a series of lectures originally written in English for delivery in America, the Shaffer (Yale) and Cole (Vanderbilt) Lectures for 1951.

"The Primitive Christian Kerygma and the Historical Jesus," trans. by C. E. Braaten and R. H. Harrisville in *The Historical Jesus and the Kerygmatic Christ* (C. E. Braaten and R. H. Harrisville, eds.; Nashville: Abingdon Press, 1964), pp. 15-42.

This is Bultmann's reply to his critics on the "question of the historical Jesus," especially to such of them as were his own pupils. It is the definitive expression of Bultmann's views of the significance of Jesus for Christian faith and proclamation.

"General Truths and Christian Proclamation," trans. by Schubert M. Ogden in Wolfhart Pannenberg *et al., History and Hermeneutic* ("Journal for Theology and the Church" No. 4; Harper Torchbook No. 254: New York: Harper & Row, 1967), pp. 153-62.

An important clarification of the relationship between Christian proclamation (the kerygma) and general truths. The first section on the nature of Christian proclamation is extremely brief and the general reader will need to supplement it with other discussions of this, for example, "New Testament and Mythology" and "The Primitive Christian Kerygma and the Historical Jesus," both mentioned above.

"The Idea of God and Modern Man," trans. by R. W. Funk in R. Bultmann *et al., Translating Theology into the Modern Age* ("Journal for Theology and the Church". No. 2; Harper Torchbook No. 252; New York: Harper & Row, 1965), pp. 83-95.

Originally published in 1963, this is Bultmann's reaction to J. A. T. Robinson's *Honest to God* and Gabriel Vahanian's *The Death of God*. It is an important supplement to "What Sense Is There to Speak of God?" (1925) mentioned above.

108

*Glauben und Verstehen,* I (1933), II (1952), III (1960), IV (1965) (Tübingen: J. C. B. Mohr [Paul Siebeck]).

Bultmann's collected essays. Volume I has as yet been translated only in part. Volume II has been translated by J. C. G. Greig as *Essays Philosophical and Theological* (New York: Macmillan, 1955). Some of the essays from Volume III are to found in *Existence and Faith.*

## More Technical Work in New Testament Studies

*The History of the Synoptic Tradition,* trans. by J. Marsh (New York: Harper & Row, 1963).

This was Bultmann's first major publication and when the original German edition appeared in 1921 it immediately established him as a leading New Testament scholar. It is one of the pioneer works of "form criticism," a method of analyzing material in the New Testament (and especially in the three Synoptic Gospels: Matthew, Mark and Luke) according to its form and its function in the preaching or in the apologetic, catechetical or liturgical activity of the early church. As the title shows, Bultmann's particular emphasis is on the history of the use of this material in the tradition of the church as this can be discerned by careful analysis of the material now found in the Synoptic Gospels.

It would be impossible to overestimate the significance of this book for contemporary New Testament scholarship. Although its influence was fought for many years, especially in England, it has gradually come to dominate scholarly work on the Gospels of Matthew, Mark and Luke. Today all effective work on these Gospels and their theology, and on the life and teaching of Jesus for which they are our only real source of information, begins with this book.

"The New Approach to the Synoptic Problem" in *Existence and Faith,* pp. 35-54. Originally published in the *Journal of Religion,* 6 (1926), 337-62.

A description of, and an apologetic for, "form criticism."

"Paul," "Romans 7 and the Anthropology of Paul," "Jesus and Paul," all translated by Schubert M. Ogden in *Existence and Faith,* pp. 111-46, 147-58, 183-201.

*The Old and the New Man in the Letters of Paul,* trans. by K. R. Crim (Richmond: John Knox Press, 1967).

Bultmann is one of the greatest interpreters of the apostle Paul, and these five essays *(The Old and the New Man* consists of three essays, one of which is a different translation of "Romans 7 and the Anthropology of Paul") are representative of his technical work in this field.

*Primitive Christianity in Its Contemporary Setting,* trans. by R. H. Fuller ("Living Age Books"; New York: Meridian Books, 1956).

The title describes this book exactly. Very important features of this work are the treatment of Jesus as belonging to Judaism and not Christianity and the description of the Gnosticism which Bultmann sees as a major factor in the background of Primitive Christianity.

*Das Evangelium des Johannes* ("Meyer Kommentar"; Göttingen: Vandenhoeck & Ruprecht, 1956).

As we have seen already, Bultmann has a great concern for the writings of John and this is his commentary on the Gospel. Together with the section on John in his *Theology of the New Testament,* it represents a major interpretation of the Johannine theology. Particular features of the commentary which have been taken up in subsequent scholarly discussion are the isolation of a "signs source" as one of the sources used by the evangelist and the claim that John must be interpreted against a Gnostic background. Bultmann's particular view of a pre-Christian Gnostic redeemer myth (the myth of a heavenly figure coming down to earth to secure salvation for men and opening a way for them into the heavenly realm) as an influence upon John has been strenuously resisted on the grounds that we have no evidence that such a myth is pre-Christian. But now recent discoveries in Egypt would seem to prove that Bultmann has been right all through the years on this matter.

## Discussions of Bultmann and His Theology

It cannot be too strongly emphasized that this present book is a nontechnical work designed to introduce the general reader to the theology of Bultmann. It is not intended to be a technical discussion of Bultmann and the issues he has raised. There are already a great many such discussions and the following is a brief list of some of the more important of them.

Bartsch, H. W. (ed.). *Kerygma and Myth,* trans. by R. H. Fuller (Harper Torchbooks No. 80; New York: Harper & Row, 1961).

110

The first volume of a series produced to record the progress of the debate sparked by Bultmann's demythologizing program. It contains three essays by Bultmann, referred to above, and five by critics of his proposal.

–––. *Kerygma and Myth II,* trans. by R. H. Fuller (London: S. P. C. K., 1962).

The second volume in the series. Among other things it includes Karl Barth's "Rudolf Bultmann—An Attempt to Understand Him."

Braaten, C. E. and Harrisville, R. A. (eds.). *Kerygma and History* (Nashville: Abingdon Press, 1962).

A collection of critical essays mostly by Lutheran theologians who stand to the right of Bultmann.

–––. *The Historical Jesus and the Kerygmatic Christ* (Nashville: Abingdon Press, 1904).

A collection of essays on the "question of the historical Jesus," that is, the twin questions of the relationship between the historical Jesus and the proclamation of the church and the significance of the historical Jesus for Christian faith. The volume includes Bultmann's reply to his own pupils, "The Primitive Christian Kerygma and the Historical Jesus."

Cobb, John B., Jr. *Living Options in Protestant Theology* (Philadelphia: Westminster Press, 1962).

Includes a very good discussion of theological existentialism in general and of Bultmann in particular.

Kegley, Charles W. (ed.). *The Theology of Rudolf Bultmann* (New York: Harper & Row, 1966).

A collection of critical essays by major European and American scholars, to each of which Bultmann writes a reply. An invaluable series of dialogues.

Oden, Thomas C. *Radical Obedience: The Ethics of Rudolf Bultmann* (Philadelphia: Westminster Press, 1964).

A good discussion of the place of ethics in Bultmann's theology, with a response by Bultmann himself.

Ogden, Schubert M. *Christ without Myth* (New York: Harper & Row, 1961).

–––. "Introduction" in *Existence and Faith, Shorter Writings of Rudolf Bultmann.*

Ogden is the most important American critic of Bultmann from a position to the left of his. His criticism has been taken very seriously by Bultmann himself and by Bultmann's pupils.

Robinson, James M. *A New Quest of the Historical Jesus* ("Studies in Biblical Theology" No. 25; Naperville: Allenson, 1959).

A description of, and a major contribution to, the "question of the historical Jesus."

Schmithals, Walter. *An Introduction to the Theology of Rudolf Bultmann,* trans. by John Bowden (Minneapolis: Augsburg Publishing House, 1968).

Much the most thorough and systematic presentation and discussion of Bultmann's theology as a whole.

Smart, James D. *The Divided Mind of Modern Theology: Karl Barth and Rudolf Bultmann 1908–1933* (Philadelphia: Westminster Press, 1967).

A description of the education of these two theological giants, of their initial sympathy for one another's position, and the gulf that eventually widened between them. The author's sympathy lies with Barth.